GOD WITHIN PROCESS

NEWMAN PRESS / Paramus, N.J./New York, N.Y./Toronto/London

GOD WITH- IN PRO- CESS

EULALIO R. BALTAZAR

Published by Newman Press
Editorial Office: 304 W. 58th St., N.Y., N.Y. 10019
Business Office: Paramus, New Jersey 07652

Printed and bound in the
United States of America

ACKNOWLEDGMENTS

Harper & Row, Publishers, Inc.: *The Phenomenon of Man* by Pierre
Teilhard de Chardin. Copyright 1955 by Editions du Seuil, Paris. Copy-
right © 1959 in the English translation by Wm. Collins Sons & Co. Ltd.,
London and Harper & Row, Publishers, Inc., New York. *The Divine Milieu*
by Pierre Teilhard de Chardin. Copyright 1957 by Editions du Seuil, Paris.
English translation copyright © 1960 by Wm. Collins Sons & Co. Ltd.,
London and Harper & Row, Publishers, Inc., New York. *The Theology
of Hope* by Jürgen Moltmann, trans. by J. W. Leitch. Copyright © 1967
by Harper & Row, Publishers, Inc., New York. *The Reality of God* by
Schubert Ogden. Copyright © 1963 by Harper & Row, Publishers, Inc.,
New York. *Old Testament Theology,* II by Gerhardt von Rad, trans. by
D. M. G. Stalker. Copyright © 1965 by Harper & Row, Publishers, Inc.,
New York. Reprinted by permission of Harper & Row, Publishers, Inc.

The Westminster Press: *Guide to the Debate about God* by David E.
Jenkins. Published in the U.S.A. by The Westminster Press, 1966. Copy-
right © D. E. Jenkins, 1966. *Christ and Time,* Revised Edition, edited by
Oscar Cullmann, trans. by Floyd V. Filson. Copyright © MCMLXIV by
W. L. Jenkins, The Westminster Press. Reprinted by permission of The
Westminster Press, Philadelphia.

Prentice-Hall, Inc.: *The Sociology of Religion* by Thomas F. O'Dea.
Copyright © 1966. Reprinted by permission of Prentice-Hall, Inc., Engle-
wood Cliffs, N.J.

Herder & Herder: *The Future of Belief* by Leslie Dewart. Copyright ©
1966. Reprinted by permission of Herder & Herder, New York.

Harcourt, Brace & World, Inc.: *Reflections on Man,* edited by Jesse
Mann and G. Kreyche. Copyright © 1966. *The Sacred and the Profane*
by Mircea Eliade, trans. by Willard Trask. Copyright © 1957. Reprinted
by permission of Harcourt, Brace & World, Inc.

CONTENTS

v

INTRODUCTION

〰 *The Future of Theological Renewal*

The most important problem in Christian rethinking today, it would seem, is the problem of God and unbelief. But any rethinking of the problem will ultimately be governed by one's view as to how rethinking in theology should be done in general. So, before I could discuss and present intelligently the subject I have proposed, it is necessary that the reader understand my position on the direction that theological renewal ought to take in order to be relevant.

Reflection on the faith is a continuing task; our formulations are never finished. Today, our world is sufficiently different from the medieval to cause a need for radical reformulation. All admit the difference, but there are those who tell the modern world to conform to the medieval so that a metaphysical outlook can be reborn and thus the loss of faith due to the irrelevance of metaphysical formulations be averted. There are others, however, who consider this move a regression, for the modern world which sees reality as evolving gives a truer picture than the static world-view of the past.

Whatever be one's preferences, it is nevertheless true that in the search for truth, both positions should be allowed to continue in their work of rethinking, for it is through trial and error and the plurality of formulations that we arrive at what is relevant, adequate and true.

For my part, I believe that the metaphysical presentation of theology has become irrelevant for the modern world and for modern man. It is not only the need of the modern world that convinces me of the inadequacy of metaphysical theology but also the nature of the faith which ought to determine the way it is formulated. The Christian faith speaks of the people of God on a pilgrimage to the eschatological Land of Truth. A metaphysical theology that looks at truths in an immutable and universal way cannot properly grasp and present the unique historical events of the journey precisely as unique and historical. Furthermore, a metaphysical outlook, being other-worldly, is unable to show the modern world a Christian outlook which values the things of earth and sees the world as in process of spiritual redemption and transformation and presents salvation as taking place here on earth. A metaphysical orientation that points to value as supratemporal and other-worldly, is to me underhumanized and not truly serious about secular values. I am forced therefore to look to secular categories of the modern world as the possible framework for theological reformulation.

The use of secular categories has resulted in various theological experiments. For example, there are those who have tried existential and personalistic categories; those who have applied linguistic analysis to biblical statements; those who have advocated the dehellenization of traditional formulations; those who have experimented with political and social categories of the secular city; those who believe in the relevance of pragmatic philosophy or Whiteheadian process philosophy, and so on. Again, experimentation should be permitted, for only by trying out all possibilities do we hope to arrive at the suitable.

But I believe that the goal of relevance is not going to be achieved as long as professional theologians (both transcendentalists and immanentists) do not adopt the processive outlook and pattern of thinking. The processive outlook accomplishes three things which I consider necessary to make theology relevant today: (1) it reconciles theology with the scientific world, (2) it reconciles immanence and transcendence, and (3) it makes theological talk relevant.

〜 Theology and the Scientific World

I believe that the task of theology is to show that its data (faith and revelation) are intrinsic to the evolving universe. For too long a time, much too long, in fact, theologians neglected the world. As David Jenkins observes, commenting on Bonhoeffer's justified critique of Barth and Bultmann, "Barth's approach (and Bultmann's too) neglected the world. But this was not biblical. It was in the world that men lived, it was in the world that Jesus lived and the Bible portrayed the world as both created and redeemed." [1] What theologians have to show if they want to be heard is the biblical view that the world is unintelligible apart from Christ.[2] The theological hang-up on the problem of the Jesus of history and the Christ of faith is irrelevant for the ordinary man whose goal is the understanding of the message of Christ and which task is theology's very purpose. Of the modern theologies, only one, and that by an "amateur" theologian, Teilhard de Chardin, has attempted to integrate Christ with the world. The theologian must talk about the world to be heard; if he talks about Christ, then, to be relevant, he must show Christ's role in the evolving universe. Here, again, Teilhard has shown Christ's role, reinterpreting the Johannine and Pauline view of Christ. We must continue the task Teilhard has begun, going beyond him, by reinterpreting the categories of sin, guilt, grace, redemption, etc. But sad to say, many, instead of highlighting the originality of Teilhard's task, have tried to "sanitize" him into orthodoxy.[3]

It is with this presently evolving world that we have to do and no other; if religion is to be relevant, its role must be shown in it. The reason why religion was relevant for the Israelites was that they saw the biblical events actually happening in their world. But for modern man, the scientific world is presented by professional theologians as theologically neutral; it is a natural order. Some theologians have relegated theology to the supernatural order; others, no longer believing in the supernatural, have reduced theology to feelings, emotions; and still others have given up on religious talk altogether. It is no wonder that modern man cannot see the relevance of theology. It is necessary for modern man to see that there is an objective theological dimension to our presently evolving world, that biblical categories are actually operative in it. But we have to know how to see. Unfortunately, the philosophical categories, existential, personalistic, linguistic and other empirical ones, are inadequate for the task of showing the relevance of religion and theology to evolution.

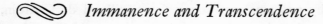 *Immanence and Transcendence*

The secularizers who use empirical categories hope that by their use, biblical categories become immanent. In the process, however, the very transcendence inherent in Christian thought has been sacrificed.[4] The result is not really surprising if one remembers that the secularizers are heirs of hellenic thought in which the transcendent is necessarily metaphysical and the immanent empirical. The giving up of the metaphysical, in this dualistic context, would necessarily entail the giving up of religion and God.[5]

Any valid effort at making Christianity relevant to the modern world must take as its starting point the tackling of the problem of reconciling immanence and transcendence. Unfortunately, ignorance by theologians of the evolutionary outlook and pattern of thinking has precluded the chance of seeing transcendence in time and history. What we have to do is somehow to fuse metaphysics and the empirical. This task is quite possible in the evolutionary context.[6] There are those who have reservations against evolution as a theological and philosophic category. I have taken account of some of these reservations in another work.[7]

Let us show then by the evolutionary pattern of thinking how we can solve the first basic problem of secularization: the reconciliation of immanence and transcendence. What does it mean to transcend? It means to go beyond a previous position such that the present one is superior to the former. But this going beyond could have two meanings, one static, the other evolutionary, depending on the context. Let us reflect on the meaning of transcendence in a static context. Suppose we had two positions A and B in which B is higher than A. We could think of A and B as two jobs, two rooms, two cars, etc. Transcendence, in this case, simply means switching to the better one. There is no problem here as long as one is willing to switch from one to the other. But suppose one likes the old one too; then there is no way of inducing him to switch. Now, this is the problem involved in the static formulation of Christian transcendence. Thus a Christian is told to leave the world for heaven, the temporal for the eternal, the secular for the spiritual and religious, reason for faith, the natural for the supernatural. But it is not easy to convince a thinking Christian that to tend to heaven is a perfection of the world, the supernatural of the natural, faith of reason, the eternal of the temporal. How can the eternal as timelessness be a perfection of time? This is not perfection but destruction or at least an abandonment of time, of history. If the Christian life is a better life than some others, then it must not be at the expense of human and earthly values. I have yet to see in modern Christian literature (theological or philosophic) an explanation as to how timelessness perfects the temporal, how faith perfects reason, how grace perfects nature, how a going beyond the world is not an abandonment of the world. The question is not an academic one. As Teilhard de Chardin observes, the dualism produced by a metaphysical formulation of Christian transcendence produces in the Christian a schizoid spirituality. Thus he says:

> I do not think I am exaggerating when I say that nine out of ten practicing Christians feel that man's work is always at the level of a "spiritual encumbrance." In spite of the practice of right intentions, and the day offered every morning to God, the general run of the faithful dimly feel that time spent at the office or the studio, in the fields or in the factory, is time diverted from prayer and adoration. It is impossible, too, to aim at the deep religious life reserved for those who have the leisure to pray or preach all day long. A few moments of the day can be salvaged for God, yes, but the best hours are absorbed, or at any rate cheapened, by material cares. Under the sway of this feeling, large numbers of Catholics lead a double or crippled life in practice; they have to step out of their human dress so as to have faith in themselves as Christians—and inferior Christians at that.[8]

For the early and medieval Christians, there was nothing wrong in withdrawing into the desert or into monasteries from the world. There was no tension or schizophrenia produced in their souls, because for them the eternal was better than the temporal, the other-worldly better than this world. The world was seen as a place of sin, error and contingency; it was not transformable, hence nothing else could be done except to flee from it. But today, the modern man sees nature as transformable; he appreciates the value of science and technology. He has come to realize time as evolutionary, as creative of novelty, as opposed to the classic view of time as negative, as going on without purpose since the universe is finished. For the modern Christian a tension is produced between his recently acquired appreciation of secular values and other-worldly formulation of his faith. How is the tension to be resolved? Are we to be totally immanentist, that is, totally identify with the secular world? But how is a Christian to be identified? How is he different from the secular humanist? The answer of some is that there is no need to, since our world is a post-Christian one. Christian transcendence is a myth; church structures therefore must go; the liturgy, God and belief, and all symbols of transcendence are out of place in the modern secular world. For the majority of concerned Christians, the tension is unresolved. They are confused and so is theology. The question remains: how resolve the tension between immanence and transcendence?

Perhaps we could affirm both secular values and Christian transcendence without being other-worldly by looking at the world as evolutionary, that is, as in process of growth. Let us then reflect on the meaning and implication of growth in the hope that it will resolve the question. We have examples of growth in the case of the seed developing into a plant, the young into the adult, the immature becoming mature. Now, in the case of positive growth, the mature or adult stage is better than the immature stage. Already in growth, the transition from one stage to another satisfies the minimal requirement for transcendence. But it might be asked here whether our example is not really the same as an earlier formulation in which the secular is abandoned for the sacred. No, because in the case of growth, we do not abandon one thing for another. Thus, the seed does not abandon itself for another seed. We have to do with one and the same seed. For a given seed to abandon itself for another would be its destruction, not its transcendence. But we can still object that even in the case of growth there is an abandonment. Upon reflection, however, growth is not an abandonment but a fulfillment. The seedling state is not a threat to and a destruction of the seed state. For in growth, the higher stage is not a destruction but a fulfillment of the lower. To remain in the lower is for the seed to tend toward death, for by the very law of its being, it must tend toward the seedling, not only to preserve itself but also to attain a fuller possession of itself.

By using the model of growth,[9] we can provisionally say that Christian transcendence could be seen as the higher evolutionary dimension of the world. Transcendence in this case would not be a going outside time but an advance into the future. But further reflection is necessary before we can with confidence accept this view.

Let us move away from this example of growth to a more formal analysis of evolutionary time. A possible difficulty for static thought is how a going beyond the present into the future can be a transcendence since the future when it arrives is just as empirical as the present. Consequently, there does not seem to be a transcendence in the sense of going beyond the empirical. So how can one attain transcendence by going into the future?

It would seem that one cannot attain transcendence by staying in time; one has to be metaphysical or metempirical. But there does not seem to be a metaphysical or metempirical region. So is not the logical thing to do to give up all manner of transcendence?

There are false assumptions in the objection just proposed that we would like to uncover, assumptions based on a static view of reality. First, it assumes that the world does not evolve, that it was created once and for all in the beginning, so that even if it tended toward the future it would remain substantially the same. In this view, of course, there is no transcendence. There is as much being before as after. In this view the world is what it is, not what it will be. The second presupposition is that time itself does not evolve, that it remains the same in the past, in the present and in the future. And third, it assumes that time is distinct from the world, that time is a container, as it were, in which objects are placed. The world is contained in time and time itself is essentially empirical and historical. The only way then for the world to transcend itself is for it to go outside this container into a metaphysical or transhistorical sphere.

In an evolving universe, however, evolutionary time is self-transcending in the sense that it transforms itself, evolving toward greater being. Thus time is at the present greater ontologically than it was in the distant past. Recall what we said above that time is one with the evolving thing. To see the evolution of time, then, one has to observe the things themselves and see whether there has been a movement from lesser being to greater being. Observing things, we find first that matter evolved from sub-atomic particles to the atom to the molecules. The molecules formed megamolecules which evolved toward the first cell. In form, in organization, in activity, in the ability to preserve itself, the cell transcends the molecule. But the evolutionary process did not stop at the unicellular organism. The process of transcendence went on, evolving multicelled organisms of greater and greater complexity, from the plant organism to the animal one. The latter transcends the plant by the possession of sense powers and feeling. But man who is a later product of the process far transcends the animal with the possession of self-consciousness and rational powers. Man in his turn evolves toward a higher level through interpersonal relationships and the historical process. It is at the point of the historical that Christian transcendence is appropriately situated.

In order to grasp better the transcendent nature of the evolutionary process, let us abstract from the things that evolve and just look at evolutionary time as a process. If one were to conceive of it simply as a line (see diagram below) that moves forward from alpha to omega, then we fail to grasp transcendence and we fall into the same difficulty that bothers metaphysicians and empiricists.

α	β	Ω
past	present	future

In the diagram, the future is just future, of equal ontological value as the past and the present. There is no transcendence here, just pure empiricism, and we would have to look outside the line for transcendence—in the region of the transhistorical.

A true representation of evolutionary time would look something like the following:

α	$\alpha\beta$	$\alpha\beta\Omega$
past	present	future

In the diagram, the future is not just itself, but contains what came before. It carries greater ontological weight than either past or present, and because of this it can serve as the foundation for transcendence.

By situating transcendent realities like God, grace, faith, religion, and revelation in the future dimension of the evolutionary process, it would seem possible to attain them without a departure from time. But further reflection on the nature of the evolutionary future is required.

Let us define more precisely here what we mean when we say that Christian transcendence is to be situated up ahead in the future. Does this mean situating it in the year 3000 A.D.? No, for this future is simply the historical future, the region of transcendence for biological realities and cultural ones such as the growth of nations and civilizations, but not the region for spiritual transcendence. Christian transcendence implies a new time dimension—the eschatological. By eschatological we do not mean "seeing each historical moment as a discrete absolute of finality," as Barth does in making eschatology the eternal that stands over time and breaks it at each juncture, or as Bultmann does in making each decision-moment the eternal now.[10]

To explain the meaning of eschatological future, it is helpful to resort to an example. Thus, in the example of the seed that is planted and begins to germinate, we can distinguish two types of future—the future before germination, and the future after germination. The days required before the seed germinates would be its simple historical future, while the time after germination is its eschatological future. The latter is not on the same level as the historical future; it is a new time dimension—the start of a new life. Similarly, the eschatological future as a theological category is a time that transcends historical time, but it should not be called suprahistorical, since there is evolutionary continuity between the historical and the eschatological futures, just as there is continuity between the seed and the plant. Furthermore, the eschatological future is not outside the historical but is somehow immanent in the historical, just as the life of the plant is somehow inchoately present in the germinating seed.

It is possible, then, through the evolutionary mode of thinking to secularize Christianity, as it were, by seeing the whole evolutionary process as already somehow participating in the eschatological Christian dimension, while at the same time preserving the transcendence of the Christian faith as precisely being the eschatological dimension of the process.[11]

∾ An Outline of Process Thought [12]

At this point, it is necessary to introduce the reader to processive thinking so that he can follow our procedure of historicizing the subject matter of our study, namely, God and belief.

Let us outline briefly Teilhard's world-view so that from it we can derive our philosophy of process. A diagram here would help:

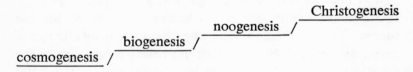

In the diagram, we observe that for Teilhard all reality tends toward Christ. Cosmogenesis is the evolution of matter whose goal is life. Life in its turn undergoes a process of evolution called biogenesis whose term is the emergence of mind or spirit in man. The evolution of spirit or mind (noogenesis) terminates in the Christian dimension which is the eschatological future of the previous stages. But this Christian dimension is still in process; hence it is a Christogenesis, whose absolute term is the Omega point: Christ.

The eschatological future is a relative term. It means the next higher dimension of a given process. Thus the eschaton of cosmogenesis is life; noogenesis the eschaton of biogenesis, and the Christian dimension the eschaton of man. The eschaton always represents the stage of maturation or fullness of being of a given process. In relation to this fullness of being, the previous stage is a becoming. Thus process or becoming terminates in being. It is justifiable therefore to speak of an ontology (being) or metaphysics of process.

Metaphysics of Process

The structure of a metaphysics of process may be outlined thus:

$$\frac{\text{(present time) becoming}}{\text{empirical}} \quad / \quad \frac{\text{being (eschatological future)}}{\text{metaphysical}}$$

Note that the metaphysical is situated in the future rather than outside time. Hence, the metaphysical is not mythical as some empiricists tend to believe. The future is metaphysical, not merely because it is beyond the present, but because it is the region of fullest being, of maturity. Second, the future is metaphysical in the sense that it is the depth of reality, whereas the present (which is the region of becoming) is the superficial and relative aspect of developing being. Third, it is metaphysical because it is the region of stability. It is stable because the process of development has arrived at its term; there is maturation and order; chance and the possibility of failure are no longer present. Fourth, the future is metaphysical because it is the region of fullest meaning, as we will later show.

What is original in process thought is the equation of the metaphysical with the eschatological future. But recall what we said earlier: the eschatological dimension is already contained somehow in its previous stages; hence the process itself can properly be called a metaphysical process. Process, then, need not necessarily be opposed to the metaphysical, for process does not necessarily mean phenomenal. Thus process metaphysics is not a destruction of metaphysics but a new understanding of it. However, process metaphysics should not be equated with traditional metaphysics in which the term metaphysical means the ahistorical, the supratemporal, the universal and the immutable. For process thought, the metaphysical is the fullness of temporality, since the future which is the region of the metaphysical is the region of the fullness of time or maturation. Hence, we do not believe (as some traditionalists claim) that Christianity is intrinsically metaphysical, if by this is meant being atemporal and otherworldly. I agree with the secularizers that we must go beyond traditional metaphysics.

Another sense in which process metaphysics differs from traditional metaphysics is that the latter situates metaphysics in the present, not in the future, since it locates being in the present, while the future is seen as the region of non-being. In process metaphysics, on the contrary, the present is the region of becoming; hence, as long as process is unfinished, we do not yet have a metaphysics. In the context of a universe in process, the option I am suggesting is not a return to traditional metaphysics but a historicizing of it by seeing it as the eschatological dimension of the universe.

My opposition to traditional metaphysics is not its predilection for transcendence, which in fact is its lasting value, so much as its identification of transcendence with the timeless. I can accept metaphysics if it is historicized. If the mark of every true philosophy is in its ability to make room for transcendence, then Platonic, Aristotelian and Thomistic philosophies are valid. In fact, if we look on transcendence as the common element in philosophy, then there is more similarity than dissimilarity, more continuity than discontinuity between traditional metaphysics and the metaphysics of process. If so, then renewal is not so much a complete break from the past, as some secularizers have been suggesting, as a new understanding of transcendence. Where before transcendence was expressed vertically, statically, now it is expressed horizontally, evolutionarily.

If transcendence is thus historicized, then a purely immanentist philosophy that denies transcendence altogether is not the only alternative to a timeless metaphysics. The secularizers are mistaken in thinking that Christianity, the sacred, the religious and the transcendent stand or fall with traditional metaphysics. Because they believed that this was so, they logically spoke of a post-religious, post-Christian, and wholly secular world, once the metaphysical was denied. Obviously, the secularizers are still imprisoned by the hellenic dualistic categories of which they are heir, and obviously they have not learned to think evolutionarily, or else they would have seen the possibility of transcendence in time.

Epistemology of Process

Let us next outline here the epistemology of process that follows from the metaphysics of process just described. Diagrammatically it would look thus:

past	present	future
non-being	becoming	being
mythical knowledge	symbolic knowledge	metaphysical knowledge

In the diagram we notice that corresponding to the level of reality is the level of knowledge. Knowledge evolves *pari passu* with being. Mythical knowledge, in the pejorative sense, is mythical because it has no real foundation; symbolic knowledge is partial knowledge because it is based on unfinished reality. It is symbolic because it corresponds to becoming, which is an indication and partial revelation of what it will be. Metaphysical knowledge attains fullness of truth and certainty because it corresponds to the fullness of being in which there is no chance of failure since being has arrived.

To attain metaphysical knowledge, both knower and known must be fully evolved. In other words, on the part of the knower (reason), to attain the future, the region of metaphysical knowledge, it must be fully evolved. As long as reason is not fully evolved, its knowledge is partial, symbolic of the fullness that it will be. On the part of the object known, it must likewise be fully evolved to reveal fully what it is. As long as it is not fully evolved, it is half concealed from itself and from the knower. It is only in the future that metaphysical knowledge is possible because there is absence of darkness, with both knower and known fully revealed to themselves and to one another.

The epistemology of process is not empirical, if by empirical is meant the absolutization of the present, for the basis of knowledge in our view is the future. Of course, in order to know the future, one must know the present and the past, but not in and for themselves, since the present and the past do not point to themselves but to the future. In other words, the present is a sign of the future, insofar as the present is unfinished. In this sense, knowledge is predictive. This is true not only in philosophy and theology but also in science. The epistemology of process is not metaphysical if by this is meant that one must go outside time in order to attain the essence of reality. It is metaphysical in the sense that one must tend toward the future, for it is in the future that the essence of a developing reality is revealed.

This epistemology produces a historicization of reason because reason attains knowledge not by going outside time but by incarnating itself in time, since knowledge as future can only be attained through the present. Reason ceases to be abstractive, atemporal, ahistorical. To be fully rational, reason must become fully temporal, earthly, historical. Reason's function is to be a light that guides evolving reality toward the future. Reason is eschatological.

◌⃝ Objective Basis of Theological Talk

We have given the reader a general idea as to how Christian transcendence could be situated in time; we have also given an introduction to the process mode of thinking to be used in our reflections. We would like to show now the objective foundation for theological talk, so as to achieve relevance.

The basic presupposition we must start with is that theology is talking about our present world simply because it is about this world that the Bible is talking. The problem, however, is that science also talks about this world. Consequently, how does one differentiate theological talk from scientific talk? Our task is to rediscover the theological dimension of the world, a dimension removed from it by traditional academic theology which abandoned the world to science. Theology must go back to the world of today and relate theological talk to everything that is going on around us and happening to us. We must go back because the world, after all, is theology's birthright. The present world is no longer the world as understood during the time of Bishop Butler and Friedrich Schleiermacher. That understanding served as the background of the theologizing of Barth and Bultmann and their followers.[13] As a result of the faulty understanding of the scientific world then as accessible only to empirical and historical method, theology desperately tried to distinguish its data from those of science by carving out a separate realm for itself: the realm of faith accessible by existential method and not by the scientific historical method (Bultmann)[14] or the givenness of the Word as a direct communication from God and hence not from the world (Barth),[15] or the Scriptures alone accessible to faith-encounter, and distinct from the world as a wholly autonomous system (Brunner).[16] Traditional Catholic theology, for its part, was undisturbed by the Protestant problem because all along it had made a distinction between the natural order as the realm of science and the supernatural order as that of theology. To make theological talk relevant, Catholic theology, in accordance with its understanding of the relation between nature and supernature, inserted theology into the scientific world as a superadded meaning. The overall result of withdrawing theology from the world has been to accord theology its autonomy by putting it in splendid isolation.

What we need to do first is to realize that our traditional distinctions between science and religion, nature and supernature, are invalid and inadequate for a true understanding of the nature of theology and theological talk. In an evolving universe we need a new view on the relation between science and religion. The traditional view makes a spatial distinction between science and religion: science has its field, the natural and historical order; theology or religion has its own, the supernatural, suprahistorical or existential order, as the case may be. But the Scriptures do not make this distinction, for they speak about the creation of this world and the New Creation; St. Paul speaks of the redemption of material creation groaning until now to be delivered; the Apocalypse speaks of the spiritual transformation of this world into the New Earth. We cannot demythologize these truths and reduce them to existential categories. Besides, existentialism restricts itself to human temporality whereas the Christian message has a cosmic perspective.[17] On the other hand, we cannot say simply that these scriptural truths are historical in the traditional sense of the term, that is, open to empirical verification. What to do?

The death-of-God theologians, linguistic theologians and urbanizers see no empirical foundation for theological talk. Being unable to locate religion and theological talk in the world they content themselves with the negative job of doing away with the other-worldly or of imposing a moratorium on theological talk. The world must be seen as wholly secular, religionless. If there is any value to religious and theological talk at all, it is purely subjective, emotive, and hence extrinsic to the world.

Our inability to situate theological talk within the evolving world is due to the static pattern of thought which both Catholic and Protestant theologians still unconsciously employ in making a distinction between science and theology. The distinction between science and religion is not spatial; there is not one area or field of the universe which is scientific and another which is theological, for science can very well show that all areas of the universe are scientific. No, the Scriptures are talking about the same world that science is talking about. But here difficulty starts for the static mind. For it, the world can have only one univocal and objective meaning. If we call this meaning scientific, then religious or theological meaning becomes poetic, mythical, emotive and subjectivistic. The solution to the crisis in theology is not solved by saying religious talk is meaningless; what the crisis means is that the static pattern of our thinking must go. But rare is the Catholic or Protestant theologian who knows how to think evolutionarily. A static pattern of thinking still unconsciously controls his theologizing. He takes lightly the observation of Teilhard that the evolutionary pattern of thinking is a general condition that must influence all theories, all hypotheses, all systems if they are to be thinkable and true.[18]

The implication of evolutionary thinking is that there are levels of meaning to one and the same reality. Incidentally, the view that there are levels of meaning to reality is quite scriptural, since New Testament writers saw deeper meaning to Old Testament history in the light of New Testament history. Are these meanings imposed? Are they subjective? Did the faith of the New Testament writers impose meanings on the facts that are not intrinsic to them? In the static pattern of thinking in which a given fact can have only one objective meaning, yes. But in the evolutionary pattern, and this I believe was the outlook of the Scriptures, there can be levels of objective meaning.

Let me illustrate the levels of meaning of a reality that evolves by the following diagram:

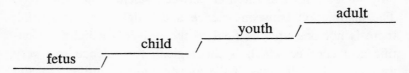

Notice in the diagram that one and the same individual has levels of meaning, all of which are objective. The individual is a fetus, a child, a youth, and an adult. This is possible because the given reality evolves; if it does not, then it can have only one objective univocal meaning. The distinction between the term "child" and the term "fetus" is not spatial, but temporal. In the static pattern of thinking, for two terms to have each an objective meaning, they must refer to two distinct individuals or realities, not to one and the same individual, for in this second case only one term is objective, and the other is metaphorical or subjective. In line with this pattern of thinking, one and the same world cannot have two objective meanings. If, as science claims (and its claims are stronger because they are verifiable empirically), the objective meaning of the world is what science says it is, then theological talk (if it claims to talk about the same world) must be metaphorical and subjective. In the effort to give objectivity to theological talk and thus autonomy to theology, the only recourse for theologians, as long as they were bound by the static pattern of thinking and its logic of meaning, was to distinguish theology spatially from science. In other words, theological talk had to refer to an area distinct from the world.

In an evolving world, there are levels of meaning. There is therefore a foundation for distinguishing scientific talk from theological talk in one and the same world. The distinction between them is not spatial but temporal. The temporal relation may be illustrated thus:

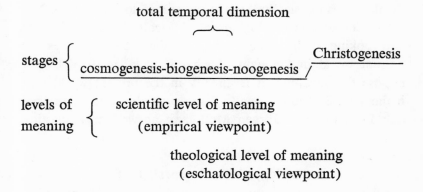

In the diagram, both science and theology are talking about the same world, but the theological is at a higher temporal dimension—the eschatological (which we have explained earlier). The theological is not supratemporal or suprahistorical, for theological meaning is not located outside this world or outside the evolutionary process. On the other hand, it is not historical in the traditional sense of the term, that is, empirically verifiable. The traditional correlative terms, historical-suprahistorical, are inadequate to distinguish the relationship between scientific and theological talk, since they are based on a static logic of meaning. Because theological talk is not empirically verifiable, it does not mean that it is therefore suprahistorical or subjective, just as the term "adult" is not suprahistorical or subjective simply because it is not empirically verifiable at the level of the fetus. We must see the universe as in process of evolution. Then we can see that it has an eschatological dimension—that, as Teilhard notes, science leads to religion.[19]

The contention of the Scriptures is precisely that this evolving universe is going to be spiritually transformed in the end. The scientist is told that his time-perspective is not the absolute perspective, that within the eschatological dimension one can see new meaning. This does not mean that the theologian is physically there in the eschatological future. No, both scientist and theologian are physically here at this time and looking at the same world. But the theologian sees the present world in the light of what it will be. He does not impose this meaning; it is already in the present world, but inchoately. But how is one to distinguish objective theological talk from utopias? Jürgen Moltmann answers this question well:

> Christian eschatology does not speak of the future as such. It sets out from a definite reality in history and announces the future of that reality, its future possibilities and its power over the future. Christian eschatology speaks of Jesus Christ and his future. It recognizes the reality of the raising of Jesus and proclaims the future of the risen Lord. Hence the question whether all future statements are grounded on the person and history of Jesus Christ provides it with the touchstone by which

to distinguish the spirit of eschatology from that of utopia.[20]

From our description of the epistemology of process we can understand how the present is symbolic of the future. The theologian looks at the present insofar as it is a sign of the future—in this case, the eschatological future, not the simple historical future. This is the scriptural view as noted by Johannes Metz:

> The word of revelation, according to most recent research, is not primarily a word of information or even a word of address, nor is it a word expressing the personal self-communication of God, but is rather a word of promise. Its statements are announcements; its preaching is the proclamation of what is to come and therefore an abrogation of what is. The principal word of promise points to the future.[21]

In sum, what we have done is to relocate the foundation of theological talk from the other-worldly realm to the eschatological future. Theological talk is thus made part of the world and is able to talk about the world—from the point of view of what it will be or ought to be.

Having given this introduction to the task I propose to do, I shall now without delay attempt to rediscover God and belief in the world. What I present is not a rehash of traditional discussion on the subject but a rethinking of God and belief in the context of process thought and of a world in process.

A Note on Process Philosophy

Some Objections to Process Thought [22]

The objections we would like to discuss are the following:

1. Evolution does not make room for revolution.

2. Evolution is too optimistic in representing reality as an uninterrupted progress. The truth, however, is that there are regressions, ups and downs in reality. Hence, reality is better represented dialectically.

3. The goal represented by your specific brand of process philosophy is a victory. It does not therefore afford room for the possibility of failure.

Our answers to the above objections are as follows:

1. There are critical thresholds in evolution which represent moments of radical change or transformation. The germination of a seed is an example of a critical threshold. In this example, there is a "destruction" of the organization of the seed and the emergence of a new organization and a resultant new life. Evolution should not be pictured as a straight line moving smoothly forward and upward or as a tree growing placidly and quietly without any critical events in its life. We should see the tree as basically the result of a "revolution"—the germination of the seed that it came from. The dynamics of germination is exemplified in the macrocosmic process. Thus the transition from the atom to the cell was a revolution.[23] Atomic and molecular structures gave way to biological structures and laws. Geological upheavals, the extinction of species, the struggle for survival and the emergence of thought in animals were all revolutions. And the emergence of man and this historical order was a revolution of the first magnitude.

There are those who see reality as a succession of revolutions that are utterly discontinuous. If they see continuity at all, they situate it within the context of discontinuity. But one has to see reality within a very wide time perspective measured in millions of years to see that there is a continuity, and that, therefore, discontinuity must be seen in the context of an overall continuity.[24] The prime category of reality is not revolution but evolution; revolution is in the context of evolution.

2. The first objection is based on the assumption that reality is composed of discontinuous and disparate events. The second objection sees discontinuity in continuity but objects to a representation of this continuity as progressive. We reply that we have to represent evolution as a forward and upward movement because we consider the evolution toward man as a forward ascent. It does not mean that there were no failures in the past or that there could not be any in the future. One must see the forward ascent in the background of the countless trials and errors, the waste, deaths and extinctions of species, etc., it took to achieve it. Thus we do not deny regressions and dips. But to represent reality as a succession of ups and downs or progressions and regressions—hence as a dialectic—is too mechanical and artificial. A too mechanistic view of reality is my basic objection to all forms of dialectic. Such an example is found in Hegel's dialectical view of reality. The truer picture of reality is that there are long periods in which the ascent is uninterrupted, followed by a short period of regression or vice versa, or again, there may be periods of dialectical regularity. These movements are unpredictable and hence not easily susceptible to being represented in terms of a neat rhythmic model like the swinging of a clock pendulum. The main movement of reality is not upward and downward or forward and backward, but a forward ascent. A dialectical view does not necessarily portray this, for there could be a dialectic within a movement whose overall direction is downward or backward. In process

thought, while dialectic is not denied, it is nevertheless subordinated to the forward ascent of evolution.

3. The third objection states that process thought does not afford room for the possibility of failure. In reply, we ask how an evolutionary view of reality could possibly ignore the possibility of failure when the evolutionary process has entropy as its traveling companion. Thus, there is the entropy at the atomic and molecular levels in the form of the loss of physical energy; then there is entropy in the form of the extinction of life at the biological level; next, there is the entropy appropriate for the level of human life, namely, human death. At the level of history there is the fall that accompanies the rise of civilizations and cultures; and at the level of the personal, entropy is manifested in the form of hate which results in spiritual death, thus destroying the highest level of unity attained by the evolutionary process—the interpersonal.

Process thought does not deny the possibility that man could destroy the billions of years of evolution by bringing it to a tragic end. It does not affirm that no matter what we do in the present, the outcome is going to be successful. Rather, process thought as a world-view presents man with a program for action in the present. It gives a framework that gives meaning and intelligibility to our present. The alternative to a processive world-view of waiting till all evidence is in is bad philosophy—if it is philosophy at all—for it paralyzes action; it lets time pass by and allows opportunities to be lost. It is fatalistic and does not give due account for the creative possibilities of man.

1

THE POSSIBILITY
OF BELIEF

Before we can speak of belief in God, it is necessary to discuss a more basic question, namely, the possibility of belief itself. As one writer has noted, "the possibility of belief itself, rather than that of theology, is the stumbling block for many thoughtful people today." [1]

Part of the lack of belief today may be attributable to a faulty and inadequate understanding of the nature of belief. Young people whose pattern of thinking is historical and secular no longer find the traditional explanations of belief as formulated in the context of a static universe significant and meaningful. In the old static framework, belief was situated in the metaphysical order, in the other-worldly; belief spoke of another world. Such a formulation was in accordance with traditional metaphysical philosophy which divided reality into two levels: the perceivable or physical level and the non-perceivable or metaphysical level. Now, this formulation was significant and meaningful for the medieval mind for whom the immutable and unchanging were of a higher value than the mutable and changing. But to modern man, for whom the historical and the secular are of greater value than the metaphysical and religious, such a formulation becomes insignificant and irrelevant. Modern man can no longer go along with the idea that to have faith, one has to abandon the historical, secular and earthly, that, in effect, he has to surrender his very humanity.

Today, the common man is being told by many secularizers that our age is a post-Christian age in the sense that we no longer believe in the metaphysical. Metaphysics in its tribal and town forms must be given up. He is told that there is no longer a transcendent God, that he actually died, or that the formulation of God by a past culture is dead, and that consequently there is no longer need for belief and that unbelief in such a God may be the more Christian way. He is told that henceforth Christianity will preach a gospel of Christian atheism and that Christianity of its nature is religionless.

The movement toward this-worldliness finds a responsive chord in modern man. However, he is not wholly satisfied with the implied conclusion that all there is exists in the present world; that all that man must work for is a family, a good job, a home, a car and all the attendent secularistic values of bourgeoisie society. There is a dissatisfaction in the young people of today; there is an inner drive, quite undefined, which looks for something much more, for something bigger than life, wider than the world, larger than culture and higher than man-made things, which their formal education has not given them. The young are looking for higher meanings and values; they are looking for fulfillment in a deeper sense than purely the material and technological which for many do not really fulfill man but rather depersonalize and alienate him from himself and others.

My own way of explaining this phenomenon is that these young people (who are most intelligent and cannot be fooled by so much sham in present society) are really looking for a meaningful faith, for a satisfying form of transcendence. But they are told that there is no longer any transcendence, no longer any faith. Consequently, they look for them in sexual love, in the sense of community, in oriental mysticism, in psychedelic experience, and so on. The main question then is whether belief itself is possible.

I do not think that the answer is in the negative and that the thing to do is to give up the search for transcendence as a myth and surrender oneself to some present and quite physical experiences. I do not think that it is quite true to say that man has come of age if this means that he no longer needs faith. I agree that man has come of age if this is taken to mean that he should no longer put much value in a presentation of belief as other-worldly or metaphysical, in the sense of the atemporal, ahistorical. But it does not follow that in saying this one also implies that one no longer needs belief. For I disagree very strongly with the hellenic view that religion is necessarily other-worldly, that to be transcendent is to go outside this world, that to believe is to be non-secular.

The task incumbent on philosophers and theologians today, it seems to me, is to formulate faith or belief in the context of an evolutionary universe. The premise we must start with is that if there is any such thing as faith or transcendence, it cannot be found by going outside time and history. If it is a higher dimension than the dimension of sensible experience, it must nevertheless still be within the context of this world.

The first step in bringing back to modern man the possibility of belief is a negative one—the destruction of the hellenic legacy of a dualistic reality. For this inherited outlook which has situated faith and religion in the other-worldly regards the world as "faithless" or religionless, as perfectly neutral and secular, and holds that any imposition of the sacred and religious on the world is a myth, a projection of the mind.

A second negative step is to give up the notion of truth as unchanging and immutable. For in line with this view, faith as the highest form of truth becomes ahistorical and non-contingent, with the result that it cannot be seen to play a role in the real historical world. It is necessary to adopt a new view of truth, the evolutionary, so that if belief or faith were really historical we would be enabled to see it.

But a more basic necessity than the evolutionary view of truth is the adoption of an evolutionary view of the universe, because without it belief cannot be shown to be intrinsic to the world and hence necessary; it can only be superadded. Let me explain what I mean. For there to be real belief and hope, the outcome must be undecided. But in the static view of the universe in which things came forth finished from God, there is really no room for true belief in the universe, since everything had its predetermined essence. There is no room for real creativity and originality, no room for real failure and chance, hence no real hoping and believing based on the very real fear of miscarriage and incompletion. In a finished universe, the activity of knowing was one of contemplation, not of foreknowledge, prediction and hypothesis. Faith itself was seen as the contemplation of truths that transcended the powers of reason.

Historically there was an advantage to the dualistic view of reality. Theologians no longer tried to impose the statements of Scripture on "poor" scientists as the normative rule for science. Scientists were left free to develop their respective fields with the use of scientific methods. But what resulted from this state of affairs was a false view of reason as being totally opposed to belief, and of the natural world as being outside the realm of belief. Later, when belief in the metaphysical gave way to belief in the value of the secular world, the predictable consequence was that to accept the secular, natural world was also to accept a world without belief, without faith.

Let us proceed to determine whether in the secular world there is any foundation for belief. Let us forget for a while belief as religious belief. Let us take belief in its widest sense, as when we use the words "I believe" in ordinary conversation. Now, implicit in this usage is the distinction between belief and knowledge. Belief implies lack of knowledge. In other words, what we believe we do not know, and, conversely, what we know we do not need to believe. Obviously, belief in the widest sense of the term is possible because there are many things we do not know. But let us consider now the more formal operations of knowing, as, for example, scientific reasoning. Clearly, belief in the sense of religious belief is out of place in scientific reasoning. There is no such thing as a Christian physics or biology. But the extreme view that there is no belief whatsoever in scientific deliberations is equally false. For great scientific discoveries have come from belief in hypotheses which were later verified. An excellent example was Einstein's theory of relativity which predicted the convertibility of matter and energy and the bending of light as it crossed a heavy planetary object. The discovery was possible because of Einstein's initial belief or hypothesis. Slowly, scientists are beginning to realize that belief is operative in scientific reasoning at least in the form of hypothesis. Modern science has not followed Aristotelian logic which starts with a self-evident major premise from which the conclusion is deduced and on which it depends. Rather, the major premise of scientific reasoning is a hypothesis to be verified, grasped by a fiduciary intention, to use the words of Michael Polanyi, or an act of belief fed by creative imagination, whose justification depends on the conclusion. Teilhard de Chardin also notes the subjective factor in scientific reasoning. For even in the process of going to the world, we already are subjectively selective. We do not just go to the world; rather, we bring with us beliefs which determine the kind of data we select.[2] The traditional distinction between reason and faith in which the scientist uses only the cold light of reason while the theologian uses the light of faith is not strictly true. John Dewey has shown us the inadequacy of this view of reason when he tells us, for example, that science is "constituted by a method of changing beliefs by means of tested inquiry as well as of arriving at them." [3] Philosophy also confirms this view of science that reasoning does not start with self-evident premises but from postulates, from pre-reflective intentions and cogitations.

Up to this point we have established the fact that inherent in the deliberations of reason is the subjective and predictive factor, that reason is hypothesis-making, that, in short, it makes acts of belief, and that in order to attain truth, belief as hypothesis-making is not only reasonable but necessary. Of course this is a long way from establishing the possibility and presence of religious belief in the world of reason and within its very structure. Our next step then is to study more deeply the nature of belief of which religious belief is an instance.

⚫ Ontological Foundation of Belief

When I believe in something, I find by reflection that intrinsic to acts of belief is the dimension of the future. In other words, belief is concerned with what will be. Belief is not concerned with what is, that is, with things in the present, with facts, for what is present is attained by conceptualization. The future, on the other hand, is attained by belief aided by imagination. Belief looks toward the future. However, it is also true that the past can be the object of belief. For example, I look to the past and I believe that such and such an event happened to me in my infancy of which I have no memory. But on closer examination, I find that even this so-called belief in the past is really reducible to belief in the future, for past events are important to me insofar as they affect my life as lived here and now. Hence, past events look toward the present which for the past is its future. Belief is thus concerned with what is absent, and this absence is an intrinsic ontological structure of reason as absent from the future.

The absence of reason from the future can be understood in two ways. In the first way, absence from the future could mean simply reason's lack of knowledge—an either complete or incomplete lack—of a reality that is already finished or fully evolved. In other words, the given reality is conceptualizable here and now, but for human reason it is not yet conceptualized, not yet known. The "future" in this case is not a temporal future but a metaphysical or other-worldly one. Such a future is the foundation for the medieval's belief whose postulate was of a finished static universe. The foundation for belief in this case would be simply reason's lack of knowledge and not the unfinished character of reality. In a finished universe, "faith could have no other role but to anticipate the correspondence of mind to reality." [4] The second way in which reason is absent from the future is not only its lack of knowledge, but the object's unfinished character. The premise is that both reason and its object are in process. Belief in this case "is not merely a stop gap for ignorance, a resting place for the human subject until such time as reason catches up. Faith is actually an operative principle in the very making of man and the world." [5]

Faith or belief in an unfinished universe is a creative principle. Since reality is in process, this implies that *becoming* is in quest of its meaning or essence. Essence is based on the fullness of being or, which comes to the same thing, fullness of development or maturation. To possess truth in this case is to possess the fullness of one's being, since being and truth are convertible. But since my full being is not yet constituted because I have not yet reached my end or omega, it follows that I do not yet have my truth. I cannot conceptualize what I am since I am not yet present to my full self. I have to believe in my future in order that I may press forward to attain it. Belief in this case is a creative principle of becoming. On the other hand, if one has already the fullness of his being, then one has also the full possession of one's essence. Since there is no longer the dimension of the future in one's being, belief ceases to exist as a creative principle.

Let us analyze further the nature of belief (and hope) in an unfinished universe. The ontological foundation of existential belief (and hope) is the unfinished character of reality of which I am part. Hope also implies the unfinished character of reality, as does belief. But while belief recognizes the openness of the future, it is hope that keeps the future recognized by belief open.[6] Despair causes the cessation of belief, while hope gives life to it. Where the end is already achieved, it is meaningless to speak of hope, or of belief, for that matter. Thus one can see that in a finished universe there is no real foundation for existential hope or belief. Everything being secure, there would be no reason to hope, believe, fear or despair. We are not trying to imply that belief in the traditional formulation was unreal or fictitious. True, belief was situated in the other-worldly realm, but even this formulation included the minimal character of belief as the absence of the object to reason. However, it lacked the true dimension of belief as eschatological, as including in its structure the unfinished and unattained future.

It is possible now, if we view reality as evolutionary, to situate belief in the world. Belief is the inherent structure of the unfinished and evolving present. Diagrammatically we have:

	being
becoming	eschatological future
present	

| region of fear, of belief, hope or despair | region of possession, hence of joy and security |

In the diagram we can see that because the present is unfinished, inherent in it is fear, hope, belief or despair. For the unfinished present to attain its fullness in the future, it is not only reasonable that it believe and hope, but it must of necessity, as the very law of its being, hope and believe; otherwise despair which takes the drive and soul out of the struggle will take over.

∽ Evolutionary Origin of Belief

Having ascertained the place of belief in the world and its role as the operative and creative principle in human striving and drive toward the future, we shall next consider its evolutionary stages and origin in order that we may realize its cosmic dimension.

Belief is not something that came out of the blue at a certain moment in history but must have evolved. For if belief is found as an inherent structure of man, then, like man, it must have come through evolution.[7] Belief must somehow be found already at the infrahuman levels. But we must know how to look back into the past in order to find belief. The principle that enables us to do so is not that of identity but of paradox. For example, if we want to look for the traces of man before he emerged, then we must not look for a miniature man (hence, not an *identical* form) any more than to look for the mature and full grown oak at its beginnings, we look for a miniature oak. Rather, we change perspective by denying the present form of the oak, that is, we must look for a non-oak form, hence, the acorn. Again, if one wants to look for consciousness in the past, then, precisely, we must deny consciousness as such and look for non-consciousness, since to look for consciousness in the form of thought at the stage of matter is to deny the very presupposition we are operating with, namely, that consciousness evolved. If consciousness were already in its present form of thought in the beginning, then there would be no need for its evolution. Hence, to look for consciousness in the beginning, one must not look for it in the form of thought, but in its non-thought form, i.e., unconscious.

Now, then, let us try to look for belief at the various levels of the evolutionary process: the rational, the irrational (animal), the vegetative, and the material. In line with the premise of continuity, if belief as an operative principle for the achievement of the future appeared in man as a "rational" or human act, it must somehow be already in the past, but in an irrational form. The irrational form of belief is found in animals as instinct. Instinct corresponds to belief and hope in us because it operates as a built-in device for the achievement of the animal's goals and ends. Without it, there would be no drive for the preservation of the species or of the individual. Instinct has been traditionally seen as the counterpart of *conceptual* reason. But this is not strictly true. For instinct does not so much look to things that are but to what will be. For attaining the present, the animal is fitted with sense organs. Sense organs are the counterpart of conceptual reason. Instinct, then, is the inchoate and rudimentary form of belief at the level of sense life. Instinct, in its turn, has its counterpart in a still more rudimentary form in vegetative life as tropism. Tropism is the almost mechanical drive in plants toward the sun (heliotropism), the earth (geotropism), water (hydrotropism), etc. Without these tropisms, vegetative life would not preserve and continue itself. And finally, if we go back all the way to matter, we find the affinity of one atom to unite with another to form molecules as the most rudimentary form of belief and hope. We might say that belief and hope are aspects of what Teilhard calls radial energy.

Let us reverse the process we took above and move up from matter to man in order to see the effect of belief as a principle of creative and radical transformation. Thus, the effect of the drive of matter forward is the qualitative transformation of the atom into the molecule and the molecule into the cell. The belief and hope of matter resulted in its radical transformation into a new and higher dimension—living matter—in which it is assured a measure of survival from the physical entropy that threatens its level of existence. Vegetative life in its turn believes and hopes in the higher level of evolution, sense life or instinct, in order that it may transcend its precarious existence in which it can neither see nor hear nor feel nor taste nor move around to flee from enemies or to seek a better environment. By believing in sense life, vegetative life was able to tend toward it and in the process was radically transformed by the attainment of a new dimension. But sense life in its turn, through instinct as its form of belief and hope, tended in its own way to become intellectual or rational belief, for instinct is unable to improve on nature. Instead of reworking and reshaping nature through the use of tools, it reshapes itself through the evolution of organs, but once these organs become specialized and fixed, adaptability to changed conditions becomes difficult and extinction of the species could result. Instinct, furthermore, is unable to direct itself consciously toward the future by foreseeing eventualities and prescribing goals. In order to survive, instinct had to believe in man. Surveying the evolution of belief, we can say that man is the fruit of the belief and hope of the infrahuman levels. In man, the infrahuman levels believe and hope that they can survive.

∾ Religious Belief: A Dimension of Evolution

So far, we have been talking about belief and hope in a very general sense, and perhaps very few would quarrel with the evolutionary view here presented of the presence of belief and hope at the infrahuman levels. But now what about religious belief? Is it intrinsic to the world or is it something superadded to it? It would seem that there is no intrinsic foundation for religious belief in the world, for does it not speak of deities, of spirits, of a beyond, of an other-worldly realm?

In order to understand the nature of religious belief, we have to change perspective. Our hellenic tradition has made us look too long at religion from the side that looks toward the other-worldly, ignoring the other side—the immanent side. It is from the immanent side that we must now try to understand religious belief. Just as once we used to look at man statically, that is, without antecedents, without evolutionary origins but instead as coming directly from above, so we still look on religion and faith. Even when historians of religion treat religion historically, they do not go far enough into the past. They still look at religion against a background of deities, demons, magic and miracles, myths and rituals, thus blinding their vision. What we should do is to shut our eyes to all these superficial aspects of religion in order to get at its evolutionary roots and origins. When we began to look at man and to study him in terms of his evolutionary past, we not only opened up a new dimension of man, but the approach revolutionized anthropology. Therefore, let us see what happens if we regard religion as the outcome of a long preparation, as a new dimension of the evolutionary process, and not as heaven-sent or as a mere projection of the human mind. We must see it as a reality that is born.

The new hypothesis we would like to present may be better understood if we situated religion within the evolutionary context thus:

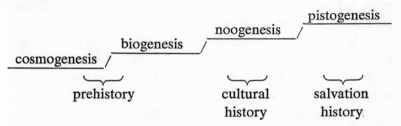

In the diagram above, we have added as the next higher dimension to noogenesis (the evolution of reason or mind) that of the evolution of faith or belief (religious). We took the liberty to use a neologism here, calling the new dimension *pistogenesis* (*pistis,* a Greek word meaning faith or belief). The dimension of pistogenesis, in our contention, is postulated by reason in process as its new dimension. Reason, we claim, evolves toward religious belief. For if, along with Teilhard, we see evolution as "primarily psychical transformation" [8] (that is, evolution as the rise of consciousness), then, at least, it should not be too hard to suppose that religious belief could be part of the psychical process, as the next dimension of the evolution of rational consciousness.

In trying to show that religious belief is part of the process, we will follow Teilhard's procedure of seeing similarities between the evolution of thought and the evolution of the lower levels. But to preclude the imposition of *a priori* evolutionary categories on the nature of religious belief, let us accept the definition of religion as given by the historians and sociologists of religion. The definition will then be related to the evolutionary process to see if there is any possibility of a fit.

Joachim Wach, a sociologist of religion, has suggested [9] four characteristics of religious experience and belief: (1) Religion "is a response to what is experienced as ultimate reality; that is, in religious experiences we reach not to any single or finite phenomenon, material or otherwise, but to what we realize as under-girding and conditioning all that constitutes our world of experience." (2) Religious experience is "a total response of the total being to what is apprehended as ultimate reality. That is, we are involved not exclusively with our mind, our affections or our will, but as integral persons." (3) Religious experience "is the most intense experience of which man is capable. That is not to say that all expression of religious experience testifies to this intensity but that, potentially, genuine religious experience is of this nature, as is instanced in conflicts between basic drives and motivations. Religious loyalty, if it is religious loyalty, wins over all other loyalties." (4) Religious experience "involves an imperative, a commitment which impels man to act."

Frederic Ferré's definition of religion contains the four points mentioned by Wach. Thus, Ferré defines religion as "the conscious desiring of whatever (if anything) is considered to be both inclusive in its bearing on one's life and primary in its importance. Or, to express the same thought (in another way): Religion is one's way of valuing most comprehensively and intensively." [10] By valuing comprehensively is meant that religious valuation is boundary-spanning; it has a domain of relevance that includes no less than the entire life of the one who holds it.[11] By intensive valuation is meant that religious valuation "must rank among the last that the valuer would be disposed to sacrifice. But even more should be added. Ideally—and definitions deal in ideals—every other valuation, including the sum of all other valuations, will, under appropriate circumstances, be sacrificed to this one. The object of religious valuing, in other words, is 'sacred.' " [12]

Following from the foregoing definition of religion are the sociological functions described by Thomas F. O'Dea: [13] (1) "It provides the emotional ground for a new *security* and firmer *identity* amid the uncertainties and impossibilities of the human condition and the flux and change of history. Through its authoritative teaching of beliefs and values, it also provides established points of reference amid the conflicts and ambiguities of human opinions and points of view." (2) "Religion sacralizes the norms and values of established society, maintaining the dominance of group goals over individual wishes, and of group disciplines over individual impulses." (3) As with the first function above, religion "affects individuals' understanding of who they are and what they are." O'Dea adds here the view of Kingsley that "religion gives the individual a sense of identity with the distant past and the limitless future. It expands his ego by making his spirit significant for the universe and the universe significant for him." [14] (4) Religion is related to the growth and maturation of the individual.

And finally, an important observation is furnished by Bronislaw Malinowski, who describes the transition from ordinary human experience to religious experience and belief as a "breaking point" to which the human organism reacts in spontaneous outbursts, and in which rudimentary modes of behavior and rudimentary beliefs are engendered.[15]

Having given the characteristics of religious experience and belief, our next step is to determine whether these characteristics conform and are analogous to the characteristics of new dimensions and transitions from one evolutionary stage to another. In general, we can summarize the characteristics of a new evolutionary dimension as follows:

1. Ultimate center of convergence. For example, the molecule is the point of convergence of myriad atoms; the cell, the convergent point of the molecule; consciousness, of life; and reason, of instinct.

2. It follows from the first point that the new dimension serves as a principle of new and higher organization. Thus, reason represents a higher form of organization for instinct; consciousness, a higher form of organization of unconscious (vegetative) life; the cell, a higher form of organization for the molecule, and so on.

3. It follows from the second point that the new dimension's new organization results in a superior law imposed on the elements or members. Thus, rational law is superior to instinct and is imposed upon the many instinctive urges in the organism as a controlling and regulative force; in the cell composed of molecules, biological law is higher than the purely physical law that governs molecules and atoms, and this biological law controls and supersedes the purely physical, in the interest of biological activities like nutrition, growth, and reproduction. These purely biological activities in their turn are in the animal governed by a higher law, that of consciousness.

4. The new dimension is the stage of maturation, integration, identity and the place of survival from the entropy found at the lower level. For example, the atom maintains itself against atomization (that is disintegration—its form of entropy) by tending toward the higher dimension in the molecule; the molecule is able to maintain itself against its

own form of disintegration in the cell through nutrition, growth and reproduction; unicellular organisms find greater hope of survival in more complex organisms endowed with sensation and instinct; and finally, the new stage of reason represents a superior form of survival, identity and integration than the lower level of instinct.

5. Lastly, the new dimension is attained by a radical transformation of those elements that evolve into it. Thus, the transition from instinct to reason results in the radical transformation of the animal into man; matter as it evolves toward the cell becomes radically transformed into living matter; and vegetative life becomes qualitatively changed into conscious life.

We can now ask: Are the characteristics of religious belief as described above in conformity with and are they analogous to the characteristics of a new evolutionary dimension? We can determine this more precisely if we relate religious belief directly to the dimension of reason. Thus, does religious belief perform for reason the functions of a new dimension? In other words, is religious belief the ultimate center of convergence and organization for reason: its stage of maturation, source of identity, place of survival? Does it radically transform reason, impose laws upon it?

To answer the foregoing questions, let us first be clear as to what we mean here by reason. Reason in the context of evolution is much more than a faculty. Reason is the term applied to that level of the evolutionary process that distinguishes it precisely from the other levels. In other words, rationality is what characterizes historical man as willing, thinking, imagining, remembering, predicting, and so forth. Reason is therefore co-extensive with man as a personal center of consciousness. Reason and person are synonymous. But it must be pointed out that the human person is not already rational, that is, human. Man must humanize himself.

Hence, reason as synonymous with man and as pointing to the new dimension attained in the evolution from animal to man, namely, the noosphere, must likewise evolve. The first men, being very close to their animal origins, were quite irrational, inhuman, savage. Man has to evolve from irrationality to rationality.

Reason like all evolutionary processes evolves toward maturation, drives toward a critical threshold where it is qualitatively transformed, for all growing realities maintain themselves only by becoming other than themselves. In order to attain qualitative transformation, reason must ramify, quantify, multiply, just as a seed in the ground must grow and swell to its full size before it becomes "transformed" into a seedling, or water increased to boiling point before it vaporizes.

To help us see better how and in what direction reason evolves, let us do a comparative study of the evolution of the lower level, that of instinct. Before instinct was qualitatively transformed into self-consciousness or reason, it had to multiply itself quantitatively. The quantitative multiplication is specific and individual. Thus, instinct multiplies itself into species—into the instinct of a squirrel which is not that of a cat nor that of an elephant.[16] Each specific instinct is multiplied individually by the multiplication of individuals of the given animal species. And in each individual, instinct is further quantified by its repeated exercise. Through these various processes of multiplication instinct hopes to become intelligence.[17] To assure this drive, the various kinds of instincts "form as a whole a kind of fan-like structure in which the higher terms on each nervure are recognised each time by a greater range of choice and depending on a better defined centre of coordination and consciousness."[18] The result of this quantification which has been going on for more than 500 million years is a rise in psychical temperature which has grown *pari passu* with the increased complication and concentration of the nervous system.[19] Teilhard illustrates the evolution of instinct toward intelligence as a growing cone where each section decreases in area constantly as it drives toward the summit until suddenly, "with another infinitesimal displacement, the surface vanishes leaving us with a point." [20] Thus, concretely, "when the anthropoid had almost reached the summit of the cone, a final effort took place along the axis. What was previously only a centred surface became a centre. By a tiny 'tangential' increase, the 'radial' was turned back on itself and so to speak took an infinite leap forward." [21]

Teilhard in the preceding paragraph describes the evolution of instinct to the new dimension of reason as a convergence of a cone into a point, or again as a doubling up of instinct, a turning back upon itself.[22] The result is the self-possession of instinct, because by doubling up it is able to possess the whole of itself. It can now look upon itself as in a mirror. There emerges reflection or self-consciousness.[23] Reflection is "the power acquired by consciousness to turn in upon itself, to take possession of itself as of an object endowed with its own particular consistence and value: no longer merely to know, but to know oneself; no longer merely to know, but to know that one knows." [24] The consequence of the radical transformation of instinct into reflection is the birth of a new dimension. As Teilhard observes, "the consequences of such a transformation are immense, visible as clearly in nature as any of the facts recorded by physics or astronomy. The being who is the object of his own reflection, in consequence of that very doubling back upon himself, becomes in a flash able to raise himself into a new sphere. In reality, another world is born." [25] The new sphere or dimension represents a new level of organization, for instinct "which heretofore had been spread out and divided over a diffuse circle of perceptions and activities, was constituted for the first time as a centre in the form of a point at which all the impressions and experiences knit themselves together and fuse into a unity that is conscious of its own organization." [26] New laws and new activities result: "Abstraction, logic, reasoned choice and inventions, mathematics, art, calculation of space and time, anxieties and dreams of love—all these activities of inner life are nothing else than the effervescence of the newly-formed centre as it explodes onto itself." [27]

The study just made of the mechanics of the evolution of instinct gives us the insight necessary into predicting that religious belief is the new dimension of reason. Reason like instinct follows basically the same pattern. First, it evolves tangentially, that is, quantitatively or horizontally, until a psychic temperature is reached, at which point there is a qualitative change, a radial evolution. Let us follow the quantitative evolution of reason. Reason multiplies itself by the multiplication of personal centers of consciousness and by the development and transmission of cultures. In the individual, reason evolves by expressing itself in many forms: perceiving, remembering, imagining, judging, reasoning, theorizing, predicting, willing, feeling, etc. Reason consolidates itself in terms of techniques, e.g., hunting, fishing, farming, handed down by the tribe to the next generation, evolving still more in terms of greater and more refined techniques and in terms of greater area of human activity; it unifies itself through the compilation of human experience not only in technique and art but in organized bodies of knowledge, the sciences, and all these achievements of reason resulting in a culture which in turn unify groups of people into cultural groups, civilizations, etc. Thus, reason tries to conquer the sphere or dimension it is in, the noosphere, just as instinct did in its own dimension. But the realm of reason opened to it includes not only the past and the present but the future. Where the world of instinct was mainly spatial, and, to a degree, temporal (it attains the past by sense memory), the world of reason is historical, which means that reason is able to perceive duration, able to foresee the future, guide activity freely and purposively, think for the first time of destiny, and fear death.

The world of reason is not only historical; it is something much wider: it is coextensive with evolution. Reason is evolution conscious of itself, as Teilhard expressed it very well.[28] Since the realm of reason is not only historical but evolutionary, the innate drive of reason is to grasp all of the historical, all of evolution, from the absolute past to the absolute future. Just as for instinct to grasp itself fully, it had to double up or be reflective, so reason if it is to grasp itself fully must double up. Reflection must be intensified, must double up, so as not only to attain self-consciousness of the present but of the whole of duration. What is this unique act of reason that corresponds to reflection in the case of instinct? Preliminarily, we can say that the act of doubling of reason must be on the level proportionate to reason, hence, on the psychical. However, it must be superior to the ordinary acts of reason like perceiving, judging, reasoning, etc. It must be as different as reflection is different from sensation and the various activities at the level of instinct. It must be an activity that can attain the whole of duration. Ordinary activities of reason, however, can attain only the present, that is, the historical future. In terms of the historical future, reason makes acts of belief: predictions about the weather, about the state of business next year, about the chances of achieving an academic degree, etc. But through these acts, reason is not able to grasp itself totally and fully, because the ultimate or eschatological future is not attained. To attain this future, reason must be reborn much as the seed is reborn. Just as the seed cannot grasp the new dimension of the seedling as is, but must give itself totally to the ground and in the process is radically transformed, so reason must give of itself totally, surrendering its very capacity for conceptualization in order that it may attain the new dimension which is unconceptualizable. The unique act that attains the new dimension and in which reason dies to itself, as it were, is religious belief. Scientific or conceptual reason is reborn to the new dimension of religion.[29]

Religious belief functions for reason as a new dimension because, being a "total response of the total being," the whole of reason is given in the act just as a seed is totally given to the ground. The result is a rebirth to a new dimension. The act of religious belief is to reason what the act of reflection is to instinct. Just as reflection is the doubling up and maturation of instinct and is the attainment of its identity and security through conscious self-direction, so the religious act is the doubling up and maturation of reason resulting in the full possession of itself. And just as reflection opens up for instinct a new and vaster dimension, a new world with its own logic, its own objects, so the act of religious belief opens up for reason a new world with its own logic and laws. Where rational reflection and laws order the multiplicity of instincts into a unity, so religious belief issues its imperative and laws to each person and to the collective entity. The religious act of belief offers a total structure of meaning; it is holistic, for within it everything occupies its proper place and is duly accounted for; it is the horizon of meaning within which rational or reflective thought operates; it provides us a reason to live and a reason to die; hence, the religious belief is a revealing structure.[30] Or again, as Joachim Wach noted, religious belief serves as undergirding for the rational world of experience, conditioning it, endowing it with consistency. Religious belief thus acts as a new principle of organization for the rational world of experience. In another and still deeper sense, religious belief is a higher principle of organization than the rational premises of reason that form organizations, because the religious premise or belief binds the whole of life and sacrifices all other values if need be for its preservation; furthermore, the religious organization transcends race, color, and other natural bases for unity.

Just as the emergence of reflection was a crucial moment, a breaking point in the world of instinct, so religious belief is a unique event of ultimate import, a breaking point and crisis in human rational experience and history, both individually and collectively. In various religions this unique event is ritualized, explained in terms of myth or intellectualized in a rational theology, but in both cases the crisis point is seen as a new birth, a new creation, a new life or existence. Or again, it is seen as a going back to the womb to be reborn, or the dying of the seed in order to attain new life, the death of the old Adam or old man and the birth of the new. In primitive cultures, the breaking point is explained as coming from without, from above—from heaven or from another world.

Finally, the religious act of belief offers identity, security and freedom to reason. Analogous to the freedom from mechanism and determinism of instinct reborn to reflection is the freedom of reason reborn to belief. It attains certainty; it is freed from doubt. This freedom is portrayed in the Christian religion as the possession of a new light—that of faith—that shows the true way to the Land, or as the freedom of the sons of God from slavery and the possession of peace. In the rite of baptism, a new identity is attained; one is given a new name.

From our analysis then of reason as process (noogenesis), we conclude that its drive is toward religious belief as a new dimension and stage in its maturation and search for fulfillment and identity. Our analysis is confirmed by Teilhard when he says: [31]

> When, in the universe in movement to which we have just awakened, we look at the temporal and spatial series diverging and amplifying themselves around and behind us like the laminae of a cone, we are perhaps engaging in pure science. But when we turn towards the summit, towards the *totality* and the *future,* we cannot help engaging in religion.
>
> Religion and science are the two conjugated faces or phases of one and the same act of complete knowledge— the only one which can embrace the past and future of evolution so as to contemplate, measure and fulfill them.
>
> In the mutual reinforcement of these two still opposed powers, in the conjunction of reason and mysticism, the human spirit is destined, by the very nature of its development, to find the uttermost degree of its penetration with the maximum of its vital force.

Contrary to the opinion of many, evolution did not tend toward reason primarily but toward religious belief, for only through belief can the final term of evolution be recognized. The operative principle of evolution is *credo et spero ut intelligam.* Contemplation or vision comes at the end of the evolutionary process when being is finally revealed. In the interim, we believe and hope; ours is the region of night and day.

The conclusion that religious belief perfects reason is hard to accept if judged in the light of primitive religions with their magic, sexual rites and human sacrifices. But one has to look at religion itself as something newly born if set in the context of the billions of years of evolution. Religion as a new dimension of the evolutionary process does not emerge an adult. In order to develop it has to ramify, multiply. In order to judge religion, we must look at its more developed forms, not at its imperfect and early stages.[32]

❦ Marxist Humanism: A Belief

Having considered the possibility of religious belief as a new dimension of evolution, it remains now to describe the types of belief that can be found in this new sphere. If religious belief is attained when reason makes a "total response of the total being to what is apprehended as the ultimate reality," such that in this act reason is reborn, then it follows that those who totally accept a given world-view as ultimate, whether it be theistic or non-theistic, naturalistic or supernaturalistic, immanentist or transcendentalist, as normative for their entire lives and as the supreme value in their hierarchy of values, and hence not taken as a means but as an end, belong to the religious dimension. In terms of this criterion, Marxist humanism is a belief. It may seem odd to classify Marxism as a religious belief, but only because we have traditionally identified religion with the theistic. But this classification is too narrow, for we would have to exclude Buddhism and Jainism too which obviously are religions. With the definition of religion given, Marxism would have to be considered a religion, at least for those who do not use it as a means to some political or economic end, but who find "in the conception of the 'dialectic of history' with its inevitability, its total relevance, its impersonal justice-making power, the object of supreme valuation and complete relevance to life. . . . For such Communists, who have sometimes proved willing to sacrifice all to this most intensive and comprehensive valuation, Communism does function religiously and is therefore for them a living religion." [33] Ignace Lepp, a Catholic convert from Communism, corroborates Ferré's view when he writes that Marxist humanists "are convinced that they possess absolute truth, and the best of them are ready to give their life for the defense and triumph of this truth. That not everyone recognizes this absolute for what it is changes nothing; psychologically speaking, a 'subjective absolute' fulfills exactly the same function as absolute truth does for those who believe in a revealed religion." [34]

But perhaps Marxists themselves might take offense and object to the classification of Marxism as a religion, especially since Marx considered religion an "opium of the people." What Marx was objecting to, however, was not religion as such, but an other-worldly formulation of religion which withdrew people from their task of social transformation.[35]

Our definition of religion and religious belief departs from the traditional one in which Marxism, naturalism, scientism and positivism are classified as ideologies, not as religion, the implication being that they are formulated and attained by pure reason alone. Yet, from the point of view of reason as a process, we discovered that so-called ideologies are not attained by pure reason alone, but primarily by an act of belief.

The advantage of our definition and classification of religion and religious beliefs is that we see atheism in a new light. It is not irreligious; in fact, it is a form of religiosity. And this fact causes us to think twice before we proclaim that the world is religionless, faithless. Perhaps dialogue between Marxists and Christians can be given a more solid justification if Marxism were seen as part of the religious dimension.

I should not be understood here as saying that all religions are the same. Since I accept the evolutionary view of religion, namely, that religion itself evolves, ramifies, differentiates itself, then there are various forms of religion that vary according to the degree that the very meaning of religion is developed in them and according to the degree that reason is reborn to the new dimension.

 ## Conclusion

Let us end our reflections on the possibility of belief with the following observations. To bring back a sense of belief to the modern world, there is need of a reformulation and broadening of our theological understanding of belief based on an evolutionary view of reality. We should assert that belief is synonymous to evolution itself. Evolution is the evolution of belief. The first basis for this statement is that if religious belief evolved, then it must have been present in the lower stages in rudimentary form. As Henri de Lubac, citing Teilhard, says: "Every belief is born of a preceding belief." [36] The second basis for the cosmic dimension of belief is the nature of the universe itself as unfinished. The third basis is biblical, namely, Paul's statement that even material creation groans and travails until now to be redeemed (Rom 8:19-22). If material creation is also to be redeemed, and redemption requires belief as a condition, then the infrahuman levels also must have some degree of belief proportionate to their level, that is, a belief that is inarticulate and implicit. In the static pattern of thought in which a concept cannot evolve, it is only metaphorically or poetically that the infrahuman levels can be said to believe.

But Paul was not being poetic when he said that the infra-human levels groan and travail until now to be redeemed, and we can add too that they pray, hope and believe. Belief evolves.

Of course, the belief of the infrahuman levels alone would be insufficient and inadequate to obtain their redemption— hence the drive toward human reason so that through it the act of belief of the lower levels can be articulated, and through man's act of belief they can participate in the fullness of redemption. If this is true, then when we make an act of religious belief, it is not we alone who make it but the whole infrahuman level with us. In that act, the infrahuman level of evolution dies with man and rises with man. The climax of belief according to the Pauline and Teilhardian view would be the act of belief of Christ as the high point of the whole evolutionary process. In that act, the whole universe dies with Christ and rises with him.

Contrary to the secularizers, faith is not banished from the world; it is reborn. Belief is natural, not supernatural.

A Note on

Freud's Notion of Religion

Freud's notion of religion, which presents religion as a way of attaining the archaic memory of the race, seems to contradict our presentation of religion here, following Teilhard, as eschatological in orientation. The death instinct or Nirvana principle according to Freud brings us to the "blissful isolation of intrauterine existence," an existence which seems to be the "prototype of the state of peace and freedom from tension, to which, in accordance with the Nirvana principle, or death instinct, it seems to be the aim of the organism to return." [37] Thus, religion seems to be a backward rather than a forward movement.

It would seem that the Scriptures verify the Freudian psychoanalytic view of religion when they symbolize religion as the "descent" of Jonah into the belly of the whale, or as the seed that must go back to the ground, or as man who must go back to the womb—examples used by no other than Christ himself. Furthermore, Christian religious practice follows the scriptural view by reliving past events of the Old Testament and commemorating the sacrifice of Christ on Calvary in the Mass.

A little reflection, however, will show that the going back to the belly of the whale or to the ground or to the womb is really a forward movement. A little reflection, I say, at least for one to whom the processive way of thinking is second nature. But for one possessed of a static outlook, it becomes a contradiction to say that an archaic movement is really a forward or eschatological one. But if one looks at religion as a process of growth, then the going back of the seed to the ground, which symbolizes the death instinct and the desire for quiescence, is not so much a going back to the *arche* but a going forward. If one stops short of the process and looks only to the movement toward the ground or to the womb as the final and absolute resting place, then, indeed, religion is a going back to the *arche*. But the dying of the seed is really a rebirth or resurrection, and the going back to the womb is really a being reborn. In fact, the Scriptures explicitly mention that the seed must die in order that it be reborn and bear much fruit, that man must go back to the womb and be reborn again. Paul applies these metaphors to the Christian religion as a dying in order to rise up with Christ (1 Cor 15:37). And even the example of Jonah in the belly of the whale speaks of the ultimate emergence of Jonah from the depths. Clearly, the germination of the seedling is a forward movement; so is birth from the womb.

Again, the Christian religious practice of going back to the Old Testament to relive the archaic events Yahweh performed on his people, a practice which was commanded by both Yahweh and Christ, is really a call for the people of God to move forward and continue the march toward the Promised Land. For the manna of the Exodus which symbolizes the eucharist (which must be celebrated repeatedly) is food for the journey. We must see religion in the context of the people of God as on an exodus in order that we can perceive the eschatological or future orientation of cult and religion.

Religion is a process of successive rebirths, and hence a forward movement. To attain rebirth, we must give the whole of ourselves as individuals and as a people to "death" so to speak, for only by the complete dying of the seed is it reborn. Accordingly, we must go back to the past to collect the whole of ourselves, for we are our history, in order that we can give the whole of ourselves in "sacrifice" and thus be reborn. This is the meaning and message of the Passover, and participation in it has the sacramental efficacy of producing rebirth; this is also the meaning of the commemoration of the sacrifice of Christ on Calvary, for by participating in the death of Christ who sums up all of the past, we also participate in his resurrection, which attains the eschatological future.

Thus the Nirvana principle of going down to the depths is just half the story about the meaning of religion. We do not deny that this aspect of religion could be empirically verified by psychoanalysis. But there is also in the depths of the unconscious the drive toward rebirth—a more powerful drive, incidentally.[38]

2

ATHEISM AND NON-CHRISTIAN RELIGIONS

In the first chapter we discussed the possibility of belief in general and we came up with the conclusion that, contrary to the traditional view, Marxist atheistic humanism is not a form of unbelief, but, paradoxically, a form of religious belief. Now we intend to discuss the nature and character of atheistic humanism and the non-Christian religions as beliefs and attempt to integrate them into a theology of religion. More specifically, we want to ask how other forms of religious belief are similar to and different from Christian belief.

The problem we have proposed is important in the practical sense, since our world is torn apart with disunity, and a partial cause of it lies in the religious attitudes of Christians toward other religious positions and humanisms. The ordinary Christian's attitudes and policies, both private and public, domestic and foreign, are predicated on the assumption that Marxist atheistic humanism is ungodly, irreligious, and an enemy of Christianity. In his mind its advocates easily become villains, simpletons, and unworthy of the kingdom of heaven. Non-Christian religions, on the other hand, are tolerated; missionaries are sent to convert their devotees. But we are learning more and more that in determining the cause of disunity, it is not the Christian's role to be self-righteous, especially if we remember how intolerant Christianity was in the past toward "unbelievers" and non-Christians. In the task of continuing dialogue between Marxists and non-Christians, on the one hand, and Christians, on the other, it is necessary for the Christian to reexamine his attitudes to see if they are not partly the cause of disunity. Since the Christian's attitude is derived basically from his theology, it is necessary to reexamine our theology of religion. Ironically, it is this branch of academic theology that is most undeveloped and in most need of rethinking.

Before the movement toward the secularization of Christianity, it was traditional in our theology of religion to distinguish Christian belief from non-Christian beliefs in terms of the so-called supernatural character of the former and the purely natural quality of the latter. Other commonly used terms to differentiate Christianity from non-Christian religions speak of the former as sacred and religious, while the latter are secular and profane. An exception was made with regard to the Jewish religion which was considered as somehow supernatural by virtue of its genetic connection with Christianity.

The implication of the difference between supernatural belief and natural belief was that the Christian, through the acceptance of a supernatural revelation by an act of supernatural faith and through baptism, was incorporated into a sacred society called the Church which had a sacred history. In this sacred society, the Christian lived a supernatural life which was maintained and increased through the performance of supernatural activities. And when the Christian died, the possession of grace (supernatural life) assured him of a supernatural existence in heaven. By way of contrast, the non-Christian, deprived of supernatural revelation, was possessed only of natural knowledge, lived his life in the secular sphere, and performed purely secular or natural activities that merited him only a natural beatitude if they were naturally good.[1] The atheist, however, being obdurate in his unbelief, was unregenerated and therefore considered unworthy even of a natural beatitude.

The foregoing distinction between the Christian, on the one hand, and the atheistic humanist and non-Christian religionists, on the other, besides being inhuman, is unChristian and untheological. With the trend toward the secularization of Christianity, the distinction between the supernatural and the natural loses much of its validity. If Christianity is truly secular in the sense that it speaks of this world—its humanization and redemption—and not of another world, then the difference between Christian and nonChristian belief must be sought within the context of the secular.

Another contributory cause to the obsolescence of our traditional theology of religion is the new consciousness in modern theology, especially as expressed by Vatican II that all men of good will, even if they are atheists or nonChristians, could be saved: "Nor does divine Providence deny the help necessary for salvation to those who, without blame on their part, have not yet arrived at an explicit knowledge of God, but who strive to live a good life, thanks to his grace." [2] This statement applies to atheists. And, in a more general statement that would include members of so-called "natural" religions, it is stated: "This [i.e., the hope of resurrection] holds true not only for Christians, but for all men of good will in whose hearts grace works in an unseen way. For, since Christ died for all men, and since the ultimate vocation of man is in fact one and divine, we ought to believe that the Holy Spirit in a manner known only to God offers to every man the possibility of being associated with this paschal mystery." [3]

Vatican II theology goes beyond traditional theology also in the fact that the salvation granted both the atheist and the non-Christian devotees of religion is not a "natural" salvation but the same salvation granted Christians.[4] But what is most significant of all in this new statement of Christian theology is that it is maintained that non-Christians are saved precisely as non-Christians—hence, the atheist *qua* atheist and the Buddhist *qua* Buddhist. Karl Rahner elaborates on this new position by saying that it will not do to reconcile the present statement with the pre-Vatican II statement by asserting that "before death these atheists become *explicit* theists on the level of their theoretical concepts and *therefore* are saved. For then these texts would simply be saying the obvious, namely, that an atheist can attain salvation if and insofar as he ceases to be one. Such an interpretation robs the texts of any serious meaning which would be worth the Council's expressing." [5]

The implication of this new theology is that we can no longer consider an atheist of long standing as either wicked or ignorant. It is implied that "there can be in the normal adult an explicit atheism of fairly long duration, even, indeed, until the end of his life, which still does not prove moral guilt," [6] presuming, of course, "that in his atheism he has not acted against his conscience." [7]

From Vatican II theology, then, we can conclude that a non-Christian of good will even if he is an atheist could be saved and that the kind of salvation is not merely a "natural" one but the same as that given to Christians. It follows that somehow the non-Christian is in the order of grace;

it follows too that atheistic humanism and non-Christian religions are not "natural," implying that they are outside the order of grace and redemption.

In terms of practical activity, the possible salvation of the non-Christian implies that secular activity understood as work in the world is not purely "natural," that is, non-salvific, nor is the world hopelessly corrupt, as some brands of theology would assert, totally incapable of procuring salvation. On the contrary, secular activity is salvific, not only for a Christian but also for a non-Christian. Salvation of a non-Christian in the world and precisely while staying in the world implies that the world which God created is good as Scripture itself says and that this goodness is not purely a natural goodness but one that belongs to the order of grace and redemption. This conclusion is supported by the Scriptures in a passage that has often been ignored or forgotten by academic theology. Thus we are told:

> When the Son of Man comes in his glory, escorted by all the angels, then he will take his seat on his throne of glory. All the nations will be assembled before him and he will separate men from one another as the shepherd separates sheep from goats. He will place the sheep on his right hand and the goats on his left. Then the King will say to those on his right hand, "Come, you whom my Father has blessed, take for your heritage the kingdom prepared for you since the foundation of the world. For I was hungry and you gave me food; I was thirsty and you gave me drink; I was a stranger and you made me welcome; naked and you clothed me, sick and you visited me, in prison and you came to see me. Then the virtuous will say to him in reply, "Lord, when did we see you a stranger and make you welcome; naked and clothed you; sick or in prison and go to see you?"

And the King will answer, "I'll tell you solemnly, insofar as you did this to one of the least of these brothers of mine, you did it to me." [8]

The important point in the passage, after making due considerations for the agricultural imagery, is the secular notion of human perfection (or salvation, to use a theological phrase) which consists in the performance of good deeds, in love for neighbor. Thus, it is not the assent to the truth of a set of theological propositions that is necessarily going to save one. The Son of Man does not hurl anathemas and excommunications to those who do not hold a given theological position. No, the one condition for salvation is how well we have performed our appointed work in the world—in short, how human we have been. To be a Christian is to be human. And true humanism is not confined to juridical Christians alone, for the passage above says that all nations are assembled and from them those who have loved their neighbors are the true sons of Man.

From the point of view of a theology of religion, however, the passage quoted above provokes some important theological questions. Thus, what happens to the meaning of the term "faith" if an atheist without explicit belief in God, but simply by his good works, is saved? Perhaps the notion of "faith" has to be broadened as we intimated in the first chapter to include not only theistic faiths but non-theistic faiths. If this is correct, what is the content of non-theistic faiths? Do they include implicitly a belief in God? Are non-theists really krypto-theists? Another question is the meaning and importance of divine revelation. What happens to the theological view that all men are saved through Christ and through his revelation if an atheist is saved without explicit belief in Christ and his revelation? Perhaps, too, the notion of revelation has to be broadened to include also belief in the world. But does this fidelity to the world and its future implicitly include belief in Christ and his revelation or not? These are some questions that we have to reflect upon in determining the place of atheism and non-Christian religions in a theology of religion.

Karl Rahner proposes a solution to the foregoing questions by explaining that non-Christians who are saved are really anonymous Christians and that their beliefs are really implicitly Christian.[9] I feel, however, that this way of categorizing them fails to give due respect to their intelligence and their freedom of conscience. I do not believe that they are saved as implicit Christians or as krypto-theists (at least, for the atheist). Let me elaborate on my position.

The central message of Scripture on salvation is that for a man to be saved, he must learn to love. This is also the basic teaching of all humanisms and non-Christian religions. Essential to the notion of love is union, which in its fullness means unity with oneself, with fellow men and with the world.

In Christianity, the perfection of man through love is understood and comprehended in terms of the category of the covenant. In its widest meaning, the covenant is man's union with the whole universe. In the scriptural view, the covenant is essential to man's very existence and fulfillment:

For the Israelites, one is born of a covenant and into a covenant, and wherever one moves in life, one makes a covenant. . . . If the covenant were dissolved existence would fall to pieces, because no soul can live an isolated life. It not only means that it cannot get along without the assistance of others; it is in direct conflict with its essence to be something apart. It can only exist as a link of a whole, and it cannot work and act without working in connection with other souls and through them.[10]

The essential meaning of the covenant, then, is union of man with nature, with others. If we compare this view of human perfection with Marxist humanism, we will be surprised to find out that although a different vocabulary is used by Marx, the same idea and insight on human perfection as union is expressed:

[Marxism] is the return of man himself as a *social*, i.e., really human, being, a complete and conscious return which assimilates all the wealth of previous development. Communism as a fully-developed naturalism is humanism and as a fully-developed humanism is naturalism. It is the *definitive* resolution of the antagonism between man and nature, and between man and man. It is the true solution of the conflict between existence and essence, between objectification and self-affirmation, between freedom and necessity, between individual and species. It is the solution of the riddle of history and knows itself to be this solution.[11]

Thus, for Marx, a fully developed humanism is a naturalism which means the union of man with man and with nature. Where the Scriptures speak of union as a covenant, Marx speaks of it as a *society*, a *communism*, and of man's essence as *social*. Where the Scriptures speak of man creating a covenant and being born into a covenant, Marx speaks of man producing society and being produced by society, as we note in the following passage:

As society itself produces *man* as *man*, so it is *produced* by him. Activity and mind are social in their content as well as in their *origin*; they are *social* activity and *social* mind. The *human* significance of nature only exists for *social* man, because only in this case is nature a *bond* with other *men,* the basis of his existence for others and of their existence for him. Only then is nature the *basis* of his own *human* experience and a vital element of human reality. The *natural* existence of man has here become his *human* existence and nature itself has become human for him. Thus *society* is the accomplished union of man with nature, the veritable resurrection of nature, the realized naturalism of man and the realized humanism of nature.[12]

An important observation to make here is that both the Christian and Marxist views of humanization are to be accomplished at some future date and are the result of human creativity. Both views portray what man will be or ought to be—hence, both are eschatological, to use a theological phrase. Both, too, are naturalistic, in the sense that human fulfillment is not something to be attained in another world but in the future. With regard to Buddhism and most Far Eastern religions, it is common knowledge that they are naturalistic, since human fulfillment for them is attained through oneness with nature.

To come then to our original question of determining the relationship between Christianity, on the one hand, and the various forms of naturalistic humanisms and non-Christian religions, on the other, perhaps the scriptural category of the covenant might prove helpful. By using this mode of thinking, we might say provisionally that Marxists, Buddhists and Christians belong to various covenants or "societies" (understood as a belief, as the context of one's supreme valuation) and that all these covenants or "societies" are various formulations of what it is to be *Man;* hence, they all participate in the ultimate and future goal: Man.

Is there a foundation in the Scriptures for speaking of

various covenants? As we noted earlier, salvation is understood in the Scriptures as the formation of covenants.[13] Scripture notes various forms of covenants: the covenant with creation and with Noah, the Abraham covenant, the Mosaic, Davidic, and Christian covenants, and finally the eschatological covenant. Each covenant has its own character, requirements, laws and prescriptions for rational human behavior and perfection. Each one demands fidelity and obligation for continuance in it.

So that we can assign the atheist or non-Christian a proper covenant, let us consider briefly the character of each covenant. The first covenant described in detail by the Scripture is the covenant with Noah. This covenant is one given to all creation; hence, offhand, it seems the most appropriate dimension in which to situate the atheist. Therefore, let us study it in greater detail, Genesis describes it thus:

> And God spoke to Noah, and to his sons with him, saying,
> And I, behold, I establish my covenant with you, and with your seed after you;
> And with every living creature that is with you, of the fowl, of the cattle, and of every beast of the earth with you; from all that go out of the ark, to every beast of the earth.
> And I will establish my covenant with you; neither shall all flesh be cut off anymore by the waters of a flood; neither shall there anymore be a flood to destroy the earth.
> And God said, This is the token of the covenant which I make between me and you and every living creature that is with you, for perpetual generations:
> I do set my bow in the cloud: and it shall be for a token of a covenant between me and the earth.

And it shall come to pass, when I bring a cloud over
the earth, that the bow shall be seen in the cloud:

And I will remember my covenant, which is between
me and you and every living creature of all flesh;
and the waters shall no more become a flood to destroy
all flesh.

And the bow shall be in the cloud; and I will look upon
it, that I may remember the everlasting covenant between God and every living creature of all flesh that
is upon the earth.

And God said unto Noah, This is the token of the
covenant which I have established between me and
all flesh that is upon the earth.[14]

The salient features of this covenant are: [15] (1) it is unilateral in character, (2) it is universal in scope, (3) it is
unconditional and everlasting, (4) no formal or particular
commandment is required as in later covenants as a condition for the bestowal of grace, and (5) there is no formal
response or ritual required of man to be in the covenant. All
that Noah is asked to do is what any man would do on the
occasion of a deluge: gather his family and animals, birds
and creeping things in specified number so as to insure the
continuation and renewal of the earth. Through this cooperation in the building of the new earth, all those in the
ark were redeemed.

We need not believe in the historical factuality of the
deluge, of the ark, and of the command to get into the ark
the male and female of each species, for these are merely
a literary way of speaking in keeping with the times. But
the central point of the revealed message is man's obligation
to be faithful to the earth, to build it and care for its future.

Before we relate atheism to the foregoing covenant, let
us briefly review the character of the succeeding covenants.
Compared to the Noah covenant which was universal in

scope, being given to all creation, the Abraham covenant which followed it was particularized, being given to Abraham and his seed. Here, there is a greater gratuity of grace and sovereignty of bestowal, resulting in greater spiritual relationship with a corresponding demand on a formal response to enter it. A defined ritual, that of circumcision is given as a sign and means of entry into the covenant, and formal obligations are needed to keep the covenant.

After the Abraham covenant came the Mosaic which is a fulfillment of the former (Ex 2:24; 3:16; 6:4-8; Pss. 105:8-12, 42-45; 106:45). Compared to its predecessor, the Mosaic covenant is still more particularized, for it is given to a specific people, the Hebrews. Here, there is a still greater bestowal of grace, greater holiness which requires greater fidelity to the covenant expressed concretely in a promise of obedience to God (Ex 24:7), and the obligations of the covenant are formalized into the Mosaic Law.

The Davidic covenant is more a transition and link between the Mosaic covenant and the covenant in Jesus than a new stage. Its ultimate reference is messianic (cf. Is 42:1, 6; 49:8; 55:3, 4: Mal 3:1, Lk 1:32, 33, Acts 2:30-36); it portrays the covenant form as the "Servant Lord."

After the Davidic covenant we have the Christian covenant established and instituted by Jesus and prolonged in his pilgrim church. And finally, there will be the eschatological covenant which marks the fullness of salvation history in which the Jesus of the incarnation will be the cosmic Christ, the Son of Man, the Second Adam; and the pilgrim church will be the New Jerusalem, present man will be a new Man, a new people. The new or eschatological covenant is the covenant of the fullness of time, the consummation of the ages (Gal 4:4; Heb 9:26); it is everlasting (Heb 13:20; 12:28). The new covenant does not destroy the previous ones, but rather brings those earlier bestowals of grace to their fullest gratuity and manifestation (Gal 3:17-22).

Paul identifies the eschatological covenant with the covenant of Jesus, and in a sense this is correct, for Jesus is a manifestation of the Messiah. Another reason for this identification was the belief in the imminent coming of the Messiah. But with our knowledge that the Second Coming is still to come and that the covenant in Jesus is still in process of being fulfilled, it is more appropriate to situate the new covenant, along with the new creation, new Jerusalem, new heaven, new people, new earth, at the eschaton. This is not to deny that the new covenant is already present in earlier covenants, but this presence is germinal and inchoate, not only in the covenant of Noah, Abraham and David, but in the present Christian covenant in Jesus. In relation to the eschatological covenant, all these covenants are old; but in another sense, since the eschatological covenant is contained in promise and inchoately in these previous covenants, we can speak of them as somehow new. Therefore, it should be not only the Christian covenant that is spoken of as new but also the other covenants. But this manner of speaking is really inaccurate and should be discouraged, especially when used to apply to the Christian covenant, for in the light of the eschatological covenant, the present Christian covenant is not yet new. The use of the term "new covenant" by the early Christians was based on the faulty hope that the Second Coming or parousia was imminent and that consequently the present covenant was practically the covenant of the parousia. We should likewise discourage the use of applying the term "old" to the covenants previous to the Christian one, since these other covenants, as was noted earlier, are everlasting in character.

In the interest of unity and ecumenism, the eschatological covenant should not be called Christian such that non-Christians who attain it are called implicit and anonymous Christians, even if, in the belief of Christians, the Omega is the cosmic Christ. The reason is that the cosmic Christ is wider than Christianity, wider than the Scriptures, and wider than the Christ of Christian theology and belief. The Omega is not the sole goal of Christians but of all men. It is necessary to delimit the term "Christian" (which after all is not even scriptural) to those who accept the Christ of Christian belief and the Scriptures and as understood in Christian theology. Christ, however, is wider than what has been said of him in the Scriptures. Christ is not the sole possession of Christians or of Christian revelation. If what we say is correct, it is possible to be a member of the Christ-Omega without being a Christian implicitly or explicitly.

With regard to the question whether an atheist is really a krypto-theist or not, a similar solution proposed above could be employed. Thus, an atheist could accept the Absolute Future or Omega and thus be saved without being a theist. For the Absolute Future or Omega is wider than theism. Theism is a particular cultural and religious formulation of the Absolute. The denial of this formulation is a relative atheism without implying also the denial of the Absolute. Thus, Buddhism has a formulation of the Absolute that is not theistic. And so is Marxist atheist humanism a non-theistic formulation of the Absolute. Therefore, if the Absolute Future or Omega is wider than the theistic formulation of it, the acceptance of Omega is not necessarily to be a krypto-theist.

Let us now attempt to complete our formulation of a theology of religion. We suggested that in order to include non-Christians in it, the scriptural category of the covenant could be most helpful and enlightening. Thus, in terms of this category, all men of good will would belong to some covenant. What must now be shown is that to belong to a covenant is to belong to the order of grace and redemption and not to the order of nature. If we can show this, then it is possible to see how a non-Christian could be saved.

Furthermore, if we could show that a non-Christian belongs to a covenant distinct and separate from the Christian covenant, then it is possible to see how he could be saved without being an implicit Christian.

That the category of the covenant implies the order of grace and redemption and not some mythical order of nature is clear from the Scriptures. Thus, it is within the covenant that one attains salvation; outside it is spiritual death.[16] The basic message of the covenant is salvation, "that God is willing to set his covenant partner in a *shalom* status." [17] When the prophets elaborated salvation history they gave as decisive points the formation of covenants.[18] Thus, for the Scriptures, God's covenants with men are always sovereign administrations of grace and of promise, specifically redemptive in purpose.[19]

All the covenants are in or belong to one single process of salvation history; hence, they are all in the order of grace and redemption. Even the creation covenant is thus in the order of grace, contrary to Catholic scholastic theology which sees the order of creation as belonging to the cosmological rather than to the redemptive or soteriological order.[20] A Scripture scholar contrasts the scholastic and the biblical view on creation in this way:

> The logical structure of Scholastic theology has assigned to the treatise on creation a place which has led us to regard that divine activity as cosmological rather than soteriological. Accordingly, it comes as something of a surprise to find a theologian like Paul describing Christ's redemptive work as a "new creation" (2 Cor 5:17). At best, we think it an arresting metaphor expressive of the novelty of the Christian order.[21]

The Old Testament views creation as soteriological or redemptive:

Because they were accustomed to consider cosmic origins as the beginning of the salvation-history, the later OT writers found it quite natural to express the eschatological salvation of the "last times," the climax of Yahweh's interventions on behalf of His chosen people, as a second and more marvelous creation. The view of Deutero-Isaias is that Yahweh will work Israel's definitive salvation *as creator* (Is 43:18-19; 48;6ff.; cf. also Is 65:17ff.), for the reason that God's creation of the universe is thought of as pertaining to the same theological category as His covenant (Is 52:15-16; cf. also Is 66:22). This conception of creation as a saving event is, I believe, the basis of the biblical view that the *eschaton* must correspond to the beginning, that eschatology, in other words, is determined by protology or ktisiology. [22]

Creation as redemptive or soteriological is a view that is continued on into the New Testament, as Stanley shows:

What is true of OT literature holds good also for that of the NT, in which the creation-theme is pressed into the service of soteriology. In fact, it may be asserted that the concept of the "new creation," together with its counterpart, the idea of regeneration or birth anew, forms the most apt expression of the salvation revealed in Jesus. Paul portrays the Christian who has, through faith and baptism, found a share in Christ's redemption, as a "new creature" or "a new creation" (Gal 6:15; 2 Cor 5:17), while the notion of "rebirth" is found applied to various aspects of Christian salvation in a series of NT writings (Mt 19:28; Jn 3:3ff.; Eph 2:4-6; 1 Jn *passim;* 1 PT 1:3, 23: 2:2).[23]

It is not only because creation is seen as a new creation that it belongs to the order of grace, but also because it is a type of baptism (which is obviously a redemptive term):

> When we turn to a consideration of the OT images exploited by the NT writers in their endeavor to describe the baptismal mystery, we find that in their works they lay under tribute almost all the great *gesta Dei* in Israel's salvation-history; the creation, the deluge, the promise to Abraham with its sign, circumcision, the exodus from Egypt, the wandering in the desert, the covenant established through Moses, together with the poignant presentation of it in the prophetic writings as Yahweh's espousals with His people.[24]

The passage just quoted also shows that the deluge (which initiates the covenant with Noah), the covenant of Abraham, of Moses, and so on, are all in the redemptive order, being various types of baptism.

It is clear then from the Scriptures that the category of the covenant is a redemptive category and that one who is in a covenant belongs to some order or dimension of grace. We might recall what we said earlier: that each covenant has its own specific character and requirement both for entry into it and for persevering in it. Our next step is to situate the different types of believers by assigning them to appropriate covenants.

In assigning the proper covenant to various groups of believers, we find no difficulty in seeing that Jews belong to the Mosaic covenant and the Christians to the covenant in Jesus. They have their respective revelations, manifestations of Yahweh, responses or faiths, commandments, morality and rites and sacraments. But when we come to assigning good atheists, Buddhists and Moslems, etc., to their proper covenant, we encounter some difficulty. However, it is not crucial for our purpose that we assign them precise covenants. God who gives the grace knows the dimension and order of grace they are in. For our purpose, it is sufficient that we are able to establish that outside the Mosaic and Christian covenants are other covenants established by God within which non-Jews and non-Christians could be saved and perfected without their necessarily accepting the Jewish or Christian faith, following its rituals, commandments and source of revelation. Nor is it necessary that we restrict the number of covenants to those mentioned in the Scriptures. For God could have made other covenants, not only with Noah or with Abraham, but also with other great religious men through whom non-Christian religions were derived. It is not necessary to go into a precise and detailed study of the origins of non-Christian religions. We will leave this task to historians of religion. From the theological standpoint, it is sufficient to say that followers of these religions could be saved because they are covered at least by the universal covenant given to Noah, a covenant given not only to all men but also to all the infrahuman levels of reality.

For the atheist, we intimated earlier that the covenant of Noah is the most appropriate context within which to situate him. In this covenant, no awareness of God is required, since it is a covenant made also to the infrahuman levels of creation. No awareness or intelligent understanding that there is a covenant or that one is making one is needed; no response is asked, no formal commandment is demanded as a condition for the bestowal of grace and redemption. All that is required is to cooperate in the continuation and preservation of life for the sake of the future of the new earth, in the case of man, and, for the infrahuman levels, merely to continue to reproduce and thus preserve, prolong and create life.

Incidentally, it seems odd to us, because of our hellenically influenced understanding of a covenant as similar to a legal contract, that God could be making a covenant with the infrahuman levels, or making one with a man who formally and explicitly affirms that there is no God. But one has to understand the meaning of a covenant biblically. Thus, the Genesis account (9:9-17) shows the essential nature of a covenant according to the *New Bible Dictionary:*

> [It] shows us more clearly than any other instance what the essential nature of a covenant is, and it advises us again how alien to the covenant-concept is any notion of compact or contract between two parties. The thought of bilateral agreement is wholly excluded. The keynote here is: "And I, behold I, am establishing my covenant with you" (Gn 9:9).[25]

Thus, we see that for the minimum requirement of a covenant, it is sufficient that God establishes it; the covenant need not be bilateral. It must be emphasized, however, that a unilateral covenant is not the ideal one, that a response would make the covenant union more intimate and the graces derived from it greater. With the minimum requirement for a covenant, even material creation can be covenanted. St. Paul shows this possibility implicitly when he says that even material creation is groaning and is in travail until now to be redeemed. Now, if redemption is through grace and grace is attained only through some covenant union, then creation, too, needs some form of covenant to be redeemed. With regard to the atheist, it would seem that he conforms to the minimum required of a man to be in a covenant. For the atheist sincerely committed to his world-view which bids him to work for a better world, to promote equality among men, to destroy alienations of all sorts, is like Noah and the men of his time who tried to preserve their world from the evils of their time (symbolized by the deluge) and to create a "new life" on earth. Just as for the men of Noah's time this was all that was required, so for the atheist, fidelity to the world and its future seems to be all that is required.

But no man today should presume to think himself saved who does the minimum, for each one must believe and live according to his "lights" given him through tradition, education and his own intelligence. Thus, it is possible to attain a higher level of covenant relationship through an explicit affirmation of God present as Ground of the evolving universe, or, as the Scriptures would say, as manifested through his handiworks in creation. This view is quite traditional. However, for traditional theology, this knowledge is purely natural knowledge, and to support this view, the passage in Romans 1:18, which states that the Gentiles can come to know God from creation, is used.

The question on the possibility of natural theology is a much discussed point in academic theology. The answer to it depends on one's definition of natural knowledge of God. Let me define here what is meant by natural knowledge without necessarily implying that some theologian accepts this definition. Thus natural knowledge of God implies two things. First, it means that this knowledge is not salvific, that it is not "supernatural," that is, that it is not in the order of grace or of redemption. Second, it means that this knowledge is attained by unaided human reason.

My position on the question of the possibility of the natural knowledge of God and of natural theology is negative. However, this denial does not imply that knowledge of God through creation is also denied. What is being denied is that this knowledge is natural. By saying this I do not mean to imply that there is no difference between knowledge of God through creation and knowledge of God through the Old and New Testaments. There is a difference, but it is not the difference between natural and supernatural knowledge. For we have already shown that creation itself is part of the redemptive or soteriological order. Therefore the knowledge of God derived from creation is salvific and redemptive, even if this knowledge is not as explicit and as elaborated as is the knowledge derived from the Scriptures. The passage of Paul in Romans must be interpreted within the scriptural view (which was certainly the view of Paul) that creation is in the soteriological, not cosmological order. We cannot impose a hellenically influenced philosophical framework to the understanding of Scripture. In fact, without this *a priori* framework it would be possible to see from the text that for Paul the knowledge of God through creation is a redemptive knowledge, since, if the loss of this knowledge and the failure to accept the law written in the heart result in a loss of grace and condemnation (Rom 1:18; 2:14-16), then the converse must be true, namely, that the possession of this knowledge means the possession of grace and therefore salvation.

The denial of natural theology is not fideism, for we are not affirming that knowledge of God is through the Scriptures alone or through faith alone (that is, as opposed to knowledge from the world). We accept knowledge of God from the world, but we claim that this is not natural or cosmological knowledge or "proof" because there is no cosmological order distinct from a redemptive order, since creation itself is in the redemptive order.

We also deny the second sense in which natural knowledge of God and natural theology are understood, namely, that unaided human reason is *de facto* able to attain to a knowledge of God. We deny to unaided reason a knowledge of God not only because there is no cosmological order from which this knowledge is derived, but also because God is not an object that can be attained through a logical process of reasoning. All true knowledge of God is attained through divine initiative, through God coming to meet reason. Reason meets God only because God has decided to manifest himself through his works, through other people, through involvement in righteous causes, through religious literature, and so on. We do not infer God; we encounter him. And in this encounter, I do not set the time and place of meeting; God does. Thus all knowledge of God is gratuitous. The so-called "proofs" of St. Anselm and of St. Thomas are not logical proofs attained by unaided reason. They are mere elaborations of the intellect of a knowledge attained by faith. Their context is a *fides quaerens intellectum* (or the context of faith), since for Anselm his ontological argument was given to the monks at Bec for their meditation (*exemplum meditandi ratione*), and for St. Thomas the "five ways" are to be found in his dogmatic work, the *Summa Theologiae*.[26]

If a knowledge of God is necessary for salvation as Paul says, how can the atheist of good will be saved? The knowledge of God that Paul speaks of is not necessarily an elaborated knowledge, a "theistic" formulation such as is found in the Scriptures and in Christian theology. It is more of the sort that the Athenians of Paul's time knew without their knowing it, so to speak, and hence an unknown God. From the evolutionary framework, we can explain this knowledge by saying that the mere affirmation of the world and its future, which is the extent of the atheist's faith, implicitly includes the Absolute Future or Omega, for the acceptance of the future of the world by working for its attainment is an implicit acceptance of Omega. This is not a krypto-theism, for, as we said earlier, the Omega is wider than theism, and therefore could be accepted by the atheist without implying that he is implicitly a theist.

One last point before we conclude this chapter is the question whether revelation is necessary for salvation. If so, it would seem that the atheist does not have any type of revelation. How then can he be saved? The presupposition in the objection is that the atheist lives his life in the natural order in which there is no "supernatural" revelation. But we have shown above that the world, or, if you will, the order of creation, is really in the order of redemption. Furthermore, creation is revelation. This assertion might come as a surprise to one who believes that revelation is synonymous to the spoken Word of God. But, again, this is a hellenically influenced view of revelation. For the Scriptures, not only the spoken Word but also the deeds of God are revelation. Revelation is a recounting of the *gesta Dei,* the salvific events of God in history. Creation is the first salvific event of the redemptive process, and hence is revelation. Thus, the acceptance of the world in the sense of being faithful to its present state and its future possibilities, working for its betterment and perfection, is an acceptance of revelation, at least in its minimal degree.

3

REASONABILITY
OF THEISTIC
BELIEF

I n the previous chapters, we tried to show the possibility and reasonability of religious belief by showing that belief, whether atheistic or theistic, is intrinsic to reason. Reason is naturally believing. In this chapter, we would like to discuss the reasonability of theistic belief, in general, and of the Christian belief in God in particular. As usual, the framework for our reflection is the evolving universe.

The secular world does not see both the presence of and the need for God today. But sincere seekers of the truth must pose the question. Of course, our day is not unique in posing the question. Humanity since its inception has always posed the God-question, but has never arrived at a consensus.

The issue between atheists and theists as to whether God is real is either an absurdity or a mystery. For it would seem that so far there has been no way available for settling the question to the satisfaction of both in spite of the claims on both sides of settling the question once and for all. Each is just as convinced of its position as the other. One side says: Wait and see; in the end you will be finally convinced that there is a God who was present all along, and without whom man could not have achieved what he now is and has. The other says: Wait and see; reason will be able to answer everything; you will then be convinced that there is no God, that there is only man.

Past attempts to settle the issue, apart from coercion and suppression, have been to accuse the other of irrationality. Thus, the atheists would say that religion is a mere illusion needed by the weak who are unable to confront the harsh realities of the world, and that, given enough time and research, science can answer all questions so that we would no longer need God as a problem solver. Religion as belief in God is an opium of the people diverting man's energies from the needful tasks of this world to an illusory heaven above; it is a projection of man's inner insecurities, and consequently must be annihilated if man must be fully himself. Religion is nothing but a form of alienation from self.

The theists, on the other hand, accuse the atheists of perverted reason, of a reason blinded by scientism and materialism. Atheists are accused as representatives of puny little man bloated with pride who dares to stand up to God to challenge him. They then try to show to the atheists proofs for the existence of God based on reason alone, so they claim.

Both approaches close all avenues to dialogue. The cardinal rule should be that both respect each other's position and believe in each other's sincerity. Granting all this, however, the absurdity, or the mystery, if you like, is that the same human reason arrives at opposite conclusions. Now, there must be something radically inadequate in this human reason which arrives at two radically opposed conclusions. It will not do to call one's reasoning the use of right reason, while the other's use of it is perverted. But neither could we say that both positions are right, for this would be for reason to contradict itself. To save reason its rationality, we must say that both positions are based on belief. Thus it is not a question of reason versus faith as a question of one belief versus another. This observation has not always been acknowledged in the past. The traditional view was that atheism employed reason alone to arrive at its position, while theism employed the aid of faith.

In the attempt to dialogue with the atheist, the theist would go outside the context of his faith and meet the atheist within the field of reason alone. But the presupposition is false, since the question of God of its very nature is in the context of belief. Whatever position one takes on it is based on belief. In the current discussions between theists and atheists, the presupposition is that in settling the question of God there be only the theist and the atheist. God could not be brought in as a third active member in the discussion, for this would be to beg the question. The assumption is that human reason alone can prove or disprove the reality of God. But can it?

In settling the question of God we must pay attention to the requirement of the "object" under discussion. The uniqueness of God precisely is to show that the atheist and theist cannot settle the question of God alone by themselves. From the point of view of reason, it is most logical that we do not beg the question under discussion. But in conforming to this requirement of reason, we have reduced God into a passive object. The setup is valid for settling problems in which the supposed issue or "fact" is within one's or both's beck and call. Let us illustrate what we mean. For example, Mr. A. says that he has a beautiful dog, and Mr. B. says, "No, I don't believe it." Then, for A to prove his case, all he has to do is whistle for his dog or get the dog and present him to B. Thus, the dog is within A's beck and call; he possesses the "fact" and is master of it. Or again, in a case in which both A and B don't have the "fact"—as, for example, that there is supposedly a new bear in the zoo—all they have to do is go to the zoo and see. The second case is really the same as the first, except that now the question is not between A and B, for neither has the fact, but between A and B, on the one hand, and the zoo keeper, on the other. In either case, some party has the fact. But now, in the question of the "fact" of God, God by presupposition is not some object within one's beck and call. He is not a possession. It would seem that the theist has the "fact," that God is in his possession. But I, as a believer, do not have God the way I possess an object, so as to have it in my power to present the object to one who wants proof. I do not possess God; he possesses me. My possession of God is more like me having a master whom I know can accomplish wonders since I have seen them, so that in a sense I possess the knowledge of them, but it is not within my power to perform them nor do I have the authority to call the master and tell him to show my friend his presence. So whether the master is real or not or whether he can do the things I claim he can is not something to be settled between myself and my friend alone. The issue depends on the will of the master to present or reveal himself, and we will just have to wait patiently for the master's own good time to reveal the "fact" and settle the question for my friend. It is the same between the theist and the atheist. They cannot just sit down, have a dialogue and hope to settle their differences by themselves. If God does not decide to reveal himself, the atheist will not see.

Many theists are really unconsciously pelagianistic when they think they can prove to a non-theist the existence of God through reason alone, for this is to presuppose that one had God at one's beck and call.[1] What is the use of a dialogue then? The purpose in entering a dialogue with atheists is not to convert them or prove them wrong about the existence of God. Explicit faith is a gift; it does not come from me to him, but from God to him. So, if he comes to believe explicitly in God, it is not I who gave the faith to him. My purpose in the dialogue is for the greater understanding, purification and clarification of both our formulations, in order that the theist be a better theist, and the atheist a better atheist. Atheism has been most helpful in purifying the theistic notion of God. God is no longer a tyrant, a God up above, a problem solver, an immovable First Cause aloof and remote from the world. The atheists in their turn are forced to strengthen their reasons for their position. And if they still oppose theism, they should oppose it for the right reasons and not because of past faulty formulations of theists.

So what I present here on the reasonability of theistic belief is for a double purpose: first, for intramural dialogue, that is, between theists, in order that we may make our theistic formulation more meaningful and relevant to the modern world, and second, for Marxist-Christian dialogue, that atheists may understand Christian theism better.

The first step in our study is a negative approach, that is, a consideration of the reasons why I think Marxism as a form of religious belief is inadequate. My critique will be from within the context of evolution and dialectic, which both the Marxists and I accept.

Marxism is a reasonable act of belief, to a degree, at least, for one who takes it as an object of supreme valuation. But I believe that its act of belief is not differentiated enough, and this I shall attempt to show, not because it does not believe in God, but because it does not achieve a total differentiation of reason. In other words, the adequacy of a religious act of belief is measured by the degree to which reason is radically transformed, since we established in the first chapter that the fulfillment of reason is in its radical transformation and rebirth through the act of religious belief.

Let us consider then what the nature of the total or radical transformation of reason ought to be so that we can decide what kind of religious belief is most adequate to achieve this true transformation.

Recall what we said earlier about the nature of qualitative transformation.[2] The notion of qualitative transformation means that a developing or evolving reality always evolves from A to non-A, since for a thing to maintain itself, it must become other than itself. Thus, for an acorn to maintain itself, it has to evolve toward the oak. Again, matter, to maintain itself in process, and thus escape entropy, evolves toward non-matter, namely, life. The evolution is from *inanimate* matter to *animate* matter. Living matter in its turn, which is purely vegetative or non-sensitive, to maintain its continued evolution is qualitatively transformed into sensitive life. And sensitive life in its turn evolves toward the super-sensitive, i.e., the irrational (instinct) becomes rational (reflective and self-conscious).

By reason of symmetry with the lower levels, and following the general law of qualitative transformation, we would expect reason as a process (noogenesis) to become qualitatively transformed. Now, the secularists, naturalistic evolutionists and Marxists do accept the evolution of reason, but I am afraid they do not know how to look for the right phenomenon which points to the direction reason is being transformed. They are much like the physicists of the past who refused to see life as the direction toward which physical, mechanical and chemical transformations were tending, or again like the biologists of old who refused to see in consciousness the direction that life was tending. In effect, they either try to reduce life to matter or consciousness to life, or they claim that in truth the evolution of matter or that of life has stopped. They refuse to see that, in the molecular world, the unique event of the germination of the cell is the true direction and goal of the evolution of matter, or that, in the biological world, the unique event of the emergence of consciousness (reflection) is the direction and goal of life. Man is still reduced to an instance of an animal instead of seeing the phenomenon of reflection as giving birth to a radically new dimension, that of the thinking layer or the noosphere. Such a view, however, is not without its principle of explanation. For in the realm of science, truth is based on the majority, not on the unique. General laws are derived statistically, based on large numbers, such that the unique is an exception. All this is true, as long as we presuppose a relatively static context in which changes are purely quantitative. But in an historical or evolutionary continuum, this scientific method is inapplicable; in fact, to see the truth of an evolving reality, the opposite of the scientific method is the true method—that is one has to look for the unique event for the truth of the process. In all processes, there is at the beginning of the process a ramification, a multiplication in large numbers, but the point to this is that ultimately there be a radical transformation. All that rise must converge. When water is heated to boiling point, the direction of the process is toward the evaporation of water. But at the moment of evaporation, the event is unique; it is not generalized.

Now, the Marxists accept qualitative transformation at the lower levels of the evolutionary process, but at the level of reason, they fail to apply the law of qualitative change. Hence, they are not Marxists enough. Thus, they see matter as having evolved toward reason, but then they see the evolution of reason itself as confined purely to the material level—from one material economic system to another which in turn conditions ideology or the superstructure of society. But this transformation of society in terms of increased material goods and a better way of life and opportunity for all is purely quantitative increase, not qualitative. All these changes are quite within the sphere of conceptual reason to grasp and to attain. A knowledge of these things will not transform reason qualitatively. One can absolutize this world-view, one can devote one's entire life to its realization, and, to a degree, reason is somehow reborn to a new dimension of religious belief, but the transformation is not complete; it does not bring reason to the fullest dimension of belief in which reason becomes radically and totally transformed. To use Teilhard's phrase, the evolution of reason envisioned by the Marxists is purely tangential, not radial. By the laws of symmetry in the evolutionary process, in terms of which inanimate matter is radically transformed into a new dimension, life, vegetative life, transformed into sense life, and sense life into rational life, so, reason, we would expect, must be transformed into something other than reason. This transformation could only be at the level of the spiritual. To refuse to give reason an opening toward the spiritual is like confining the growth of the acorn to being a super-acorn without its ever becoming an oak. The qualitative transformation which the Marxists allow from one economic structure to another: from slave society to the feudalistic, from the feudalistic to the capitalistic, and from the capitalistic to the communistic (supposedly), is, in terms of the evolution of reason, merely quantitative change.

For many, the suprarational as the true direction for reason's qualitative transformation is automatically disqualified as a possibility because of its supposedly supratemporal and other-worldly character. But as we have shown in the previous chapter, religious belief in which a spiritual belief can take place is an evolutionary dimension of reality. Of course, one could still deny the suprarational as the true direction, but it should not be for the reason that it is other-worldly. Spiritual belief or faith is an evolutionary level beyond rational experience. That it is the true direction for reason is confirmed from the fact that at the lower levels the true direction is always toward a level that is beyond the awareness, grasp or measure of that which is being transformed. Thus, rationality which is the direction of the evolution of instinct is beyond the sense experience of animals, and life which is the goal of the evolution of matter is beyond the measure and laws of matter. If these observations are true, then the communist utopia of full material prosperity and superabundance which is well within the conceptual experience of reason is not the goal for the radical and qualitative transformation of reason. The vision of an indefinite progress and increase in technology, rational and social organization, is like the indefinite extension of a line, hence, still a one-dimensional change, whereas what is demanded is the qualitative transformation of the line into a surface, so as to attain a true infinite or a new dimension. I do not deny that, to a degree, Marxist humanism is able to humanize man, but I believe that it does not fully humanize him. I will even admit that Marxist humanism in its very acceptance of and fidelity to the world and man contains an implicit spiritual faith, but I think that Marxist belief is underdeveloped, undifferentiated.

In my view, the Christian faith satisfies the requirement needed for the full qualitative transformation of reason, first because faith is a new dimension that transcends conceptual reason and to which reason is reborn to the spiritual. Second, the Christian faith offers man something bigger than life, something greater than man-made things like culture and technology. It offers true transcendence in the spiritual transformation of both reason and the world.

If the Christian faith is the fulfillment of reason, then it has the truth about the world. Methodologically, then, it is from faith that I shall try to understand the world. But my understanding of the faith is set in the context of an evolving universe; therefore, it is from this total context that I try to show the reasonability of my theistic belief and the inadequacy of atheism and other forms of theism, a task to which I shall now address myself.

I shall begin by saying that I no longer find the so-called traditional "proofs" for God's existence meaningful for clarifying my belief in God. I go along with Nietzsche, Feuerbach, Marx and Sartre and the modern death-of-God theologians that the God of traditional metaphysics is dead, and that in relation to this formulation, it is more Christian to be atheistic than theistic. My main reason for giving up the traditional arguments is that I no longer believe in a dualistic framework in which these arguments were derived. But for that matter, I do not quite accept the "atheism" of Marx or of the death-of-God theologians for the very same reason, namely, that their counterarguments against traditional theism also take their point of departure from the dualistic framework.

Let us briefly review some representative arguments for the reality of God, not to make a critique of the arguments themselves, but to show the dualistic framework as their point of departure.

For the mind of a Platonic cast, the ideal was more real than the real, more other-worldly than worldly. Consequently, for Augustine, Anselm, Descartes and Leibniz, God was situated in the ideal order. The starting point for the search for God was in reason itself, since it was most akin to the pure ideas and because reason was considered to be in the ideal order. Faith in God was formulated intellectually as an Idea in reason to be intuited or illuminated. But St. Thomas considered these idealistic arguments illegitimate since it was a fallacy, he claimed, to make a transition from the ideal to the real order. For St. Thomas, the starting point was the cosmological order. He explained his belief in God by using the basic argument from contingency which postulates an Efficient Cause. But he, like his predecessors, tried to locate God beyond the contingent, except that this beyond was no longer the ideal but the metaphysical. In both cases, God was protected from contingency and change by being situated in the region of atemporality and ahistoricity. There were objections made against these "proofs" like the one made by Kant who noted that one cannot argue from finite causes to the Infinite Cause, because from the finite all one gets is the finite.

Hegel tried to bridge the ideal and the cosmological orders by identifying God with both. For Hegel, God was an *a priori* presupposition of his philosophy. In the Hegelian dialectic, God as Idea had to externalize itself into Nature (Man) which then must be negated in order that the third moment, the Absolute Spirit, may emerge and be fulfilled. In the end, however, idealism triumphs. Marx, following Feuerbach, rebelled against the ideal God of Hegel because it drew men away from the world. Instead of an ideal God, Marx presents us with man alone as God.

In more recent times, neo-classical theism (Whiteheadian process philosophy and theology) has reacted against the remote, transcendent, immutable and uninvolved God of classicism by making God totally immanent as evolving Deity.

And lastly, the modern secularizers consider the notion of God as essentially metaphysical. Therefore, in doing away with metaphysics, they also do away with God, either actually as an event or culturally as a notion and formulation.

Now, from the very sketchy review made of thought on God, we observe that they all stem from the same dualistic tradition. The atheism of Marxism and of the modern secularizers is really the choosing of one side of the dualism, while the theism of the traditionalists is the choosing of the other side. But if the dualism is false, then not only the theistic formulation but also the atheistic position becomes irrelevant and insignificant. The assumption of the secularizers and the atheists that the reality of God stands or falls with the reality of metaphysics is false.

I believe that the correct context for thinking about God is the evolutionary context, that is, the world in process. In starting with the evolving world, I do not presuppose like the naturalists or Marxists that the world is self-sufficient, i.e., that it has all the powers needed to evolve itself, for this presupposition which is really nothing else but the notion of an Aristotelian nature has not really transcended the dualism of a natural and a supernatural order.

God as Ground of Evolution

Now those who accept the evolutionary perspective are generally agreed that the universe is one single process and that there are stages in the process: the evolution of matter, next the emergence of the first unicellular organisms, then a process of further evolution of life toward vegetative and animal life, and from this latter phase emerged man.

By studying the nature of the process, a scientist might argue that he can make sense out of the evolutionary process without the postulate of God. I agree that the scientist does not need the God-postulate. In fact, if he is to be true to the scientific method, he cannot bring God into the picture even if he wanted to, for by the methods of science, there is no way of verifying whether God is present or not. The scientist as scientist does not make a choice for or against God. But one cannot extrapolate the method of science and make it an absolute criterion for deciding the God-question and making the assertion that the universe is self-sufficient. For in so doing, one has begun to exceed the competence of science, inasmuch as such a statement is not scientific but philosophic, and to accept the statements of science as universal facts is scientism.

The notion of a self-sufficient and self-transcendent universe is not a scientific notion but a philosophic and theological one, that is, one based on a postulate or presupposition not susceptible to empirical verification. We can determine however whether it makes philosophical sense or not. Now I find difficulty with this notion. Self-transcendence, I take it, does not mean the mere explicitation of a reality implicit in the beginning but rather the creation of novelty. If this is the case, then one is faced with the problem of explaining how the higher level of one and the same process came from the lower level without denying at the same time the principle of causality. In reply, it might be answered that the distinction between a higher and a lower stage is an abstraction, since in process concretely taken, there is only the self-transcending process without a lower and a higher stage. However, if we believe seriously in time, then there must have been a time when this self-transcending process did not have the present higher stage of being. If so, how could it have attained this stage? It could, it might be argued, precisely because it is of the nature of this process to transcend itself. In support of this contention, it might be pointed out to me that we can argue by analogy to the self-transcendence of the universe from instances of transcendence which can be empirically verified. Thus, an empirical and first-hand evidence of self-transcendance would be my own experience as a self-transcending being. But this argument really begs the question, since it is being presupposed that my experience is one of self-transcendence, that is, as solely caused by me and not through the cooperation of another.

Another line of argument in support of the notion of the self-sufficiency and self-transcendence of the universe, and hence of the uselessness of the God-postulate, is the experience of duration. I will be told to experience process in its totality and not cut it up into past, present and future. What I am being asked, in other words, is to see the process timelessly.

But is this not a static view of process, in which there is really no becoming and creativity? In fact, is it not a more static view than the Aristotelian view of becoming which sees everything that comes forth as already precontained in the beginning, for this latter, at least, allows for a becoming, whereas in the former, there is a mere juxtaposition of one stage with the other?

From a mere reflection on the notion of evolution, it is not easy to see the contradiction in the notion of a self-transcendent and self-sufficient universe. Therefore, let us take examples of development and see whether or not the notion of self-transcendence or self-sufficiency is verified. Let us take the simple case of a seed that germinates, grows and bears fruit. Now, this seems to be a perfect example of a self-transcending and self-sufficient process. The seed seems to be able to evolve itself into a plant; the plant is able to flower and bear fruit, all by itself without the help of another plant. It would seem that it had all the natural powers within it from the beginning to attain its natural end of bearing fruit. In short, it is an autonomous, independent, and self-functioning unit; it is an organism. From this superficial observation, it is easy to make the extrapolation and argue that the universe is like an organism that is self-sufficient, self-transcending. But upon closer examination we realize that the seed alone by itself apart from the ground cannot really evolve itself. The seed left alone on the table will not evolve, cannot transcend itself. It has need of the soil, moisture, air, sunlight, etc.—in short, of its "ground" or "other." Call the "ground" a condition; if you will, call it cause. The fact is, the "ground" is necessary to the development of the seed. What is true of the seed is true of the fetus. Thus, the fetus has need of the womb as its "ground" or "other." Again, the living organism has need of its environment; the human "I" has need of its "Thou."

In the context of evolution, being always needs an "other." There is no process we are aware of that does not require an "other." If this is true, then why should we now make an exception in the case of the macrocosmic process and say that it is self-sufficient, that it has no need of its own proper ground or "other"? Could it be perhaps because of our inherited legacy from hellenic thought which makes us see things as substances or natures that are self-sufficient? Could it be because of our scientific and philosophic method of examining things as specimens, forms? Or could it be because of our habit of "defining" things by cutting them off, separating and abstracting them from an undifferentiated whole?

However, the law of an evolutionary universe is that, at all levels, independence is attained through union, hence, through another. No being is an island. The more the seed unites itself with the ground, the more it sinks its roots in it, the more it attains differentiation and thus self-sufficiency. On the other hand, if it separates itself from the ground, it does not attain differentiation and independence because it begins to shrivel up and die. The same is true for the fetus, for the living organism in relation to its environment, for the human "I" in relation to the "Thou." But let us examine all the levels of the evolutionary process to see if there is any exception to the law that self-sufficiency and self-transcendence are not in going it alone but in union. Thus, at the lowest level, electrons tend to unite and converge in the atom; atoms converge by molecularization, crystallization; molecules unite by polymerization; cells unite by conjugation, reproduction, association; nerve ganglions concentrate and localize to form a brain by what might be called a process of cephalization; the higher animal groups form colonies, hives, herds, societies, etc.; man socializes and forms civilizations as foci of attraction and organization. Teilhard de Chardin admirably sums up the universal law that transcendence is in union thus:

In any domain—whether it be the cells of a body, the members of a society or the elements of a spiritual synthesis—union differentiates. In every organized whole, the parts perfect themselves and fulfill themselves. Through neglect of this universal rule many a system of pantheism has led us astray to the cult of a great All in which individuals were supposed to be merged like a drop in the ocean or like a dissolving grain of salt. Applied to the case of the summation of consciousnesses, the law of union rids us of this perilous and recurrent illusion. No, following the confluent orbits of their centers, the grains of consciousness do not tend to lose their outlines and blend, but, on the contrary, to accentuate the depth and incommunicability of their egos. The more "other" they become in conjunction, the more they find themselves as "self." [3]

Now, those who believe in the macrocosmic process as a self-sufficient process might well concede that among parts of the universe union differentiates, that the law of transcendence is in union, but they do not see the need or cogency of applying this law to the universe itself. For they could well argue that what the parts cannot do, the whole can do. Thus, for example, they can show that what a single cell cannot do by itself, the body of which it is part can do. This argument, however, falls, because we have shown that although a body, say, a plant, can accomplish what the individual cells in it cannot do, e.g., flower and bear fruit, still, the plant needs the ground as its "other." The plant, as a whole, is self-sufficient *relative* to the parts, but not in the absolute sense of not needing an "other." Similarly, while it is true that the universe as a whole can accomplish what its parts cannot do, this does not imply absolute self-sufficiency but merely relative self-sufficiency. There is no justifiable reason why we should make an exception in the case of the universe to the universal law that anything that grows needs an "other."

Some atheists and naturalists usually base their argument for self-sufficiency and self-transcendence on man's feeling of mastery of himself and of the universe. Man's accomplishments are recounted and paraded before us. But this argument based on historical evidence is inconclusive because for every good deed or accomplishment, we could put alongside it an evil deed. Man as an individual and as a collective is composed of lights and shadows; he alternates between feelings of helplessness and of power. Every age has its pessimists and optimists. We cannot prove from historical evidence who is right. Thus, the argument based on the feelings, temperament and mood of an age is inconclusive. A solid argument should be based on something intellectual. Thus, an atheist or naturalist could argue that man does not need God as an "Other" or Ground because man's "other" is other men or the community—the classless community of the communists' Utopia. That ideal community is slowly being achieved and it is being achieved by man alone. The God-postulate is not necessary to solve our human problems. Now, this argument is an intellectual argument and deserves an intellectual analysis.

That man's "other" is other men or the community seems quite convincing until it is submitted to the law of symmetry found on all levels of the evolving universe. In order to determine whether man's "other" is other men, we should go to the lower levels of evolution to learn what otherness is and means for things that grow and evolve. Now, at the lower level we find that the "other" of the molecule is not another molecule but the cell. In other words, the "other" of non-life is not non-life but life. Or, again, to use a more familiar example, the "other" of a seed is not another seed; it is not even a super-seed, or a "community" of seeds but a non-seed, that is, the ground. Accordingly, it would be against the symmetry of the evolutionary process to say that the "other" of man is other men. If the seed's "other" is a non-seed (the soil), so we would expect by reason of symmetry that the "other" of man would be other-than-human, as other as the ground is from the seed, and not the otherness of a "super-seed" from an ordinary seed. Hence, the "other" of man is not a superman.

Part of the difficulty in seeing the need for a Ground to the evolutionary process is that this Ground is not perceivable. Added to this is the inability of the common man to think paradoxically or in a polarized manner. When he is told to think of otherness, it is usually an other but within the same kind or species. Thus, the "other" of a seed is another seed; of man, another man. It is necessary to use polar or paradoxical thinking, for this is the very requirement of the "object" we are trying to understand. Without this pre-condition, we would be imposing false conditions and demands on the "object" before we see and accept it. It would be like the seed demanding that for it to accept the existence and reality of the ground, it be seen as another seed or as a plant. Clearly, the false presupposition precludes the chance for a correct answer.

God is not a being among other beings any more than the ground is a seed among seeds. The ground is in a totally different dimension, and hence unperceivable, so to speak, from the seed's point of view. Just as the seed must learn to see beyond the world of the seed, beyond the forms and objects found there, so reason must learn to see beyond its world, beyond its logic, beyond the forms and objects found in it, for its "Other" and Ground. But here difficulty again confronts the atheist or naturalist, for when he hears someone speak of God as the Beyond, he immediately conjures up in his mind an other-worldly Being, a Being beyond this world. But the term "beyond" does not necessarily mean separation or remoteness. The ground is beyond or outside the world of the seed, it is true, but this does not mean separation or remoteness, for clearly, the ground is the presupposition of the seed; it is its ground, precisely, and hence its "within," so to speak, more immanent than the seed is to itself, for the seed is unthinkable apart from the ground; its very structuring (morphological, physiological, teleological) is for the ground. Similarly, God as the Ground of evolution is really the "Within" of the universe, its depth, if you will, more immanent to the universe than the universe is to itself, such that the universe is unthinkable apart from it, and yet, paradoxically, is not part of the universe. The inadequacy of the atheistic and naturalistic outlooks, it seems to me, is that they are "short-sighted." They take as their basic postulate that the meaning of the universe can be found only within itself; they rule out beforehand any transcendent source. But, again, this is like the seed trying to explain itself by itself, ruling out any explanation of itself beyond itself.

∽ God as Ground-Alpha or Creator-Ground

Our previous argument for the need of a Ground was based on our analysis of the notion of growth, namely, that anything that grows needs a ground. Let us now introduce another argument to show the relevance of God to the universe by using the evolutionary category of birth.

Birth is an essential condition of all things in process. In other words, in an evolving universe, everything comes to be by birth. Even the universe is born. As Teilhard observes, the "universe . . . places itself among the realities which are born, which grow, and which die." [4] Now, obviously, from all instances of birth, nothing gives birth to itself but must be born from another. Thus, if the universe is born, then it must have come from a Creator who gave it being. If this is true, then the argument that the universe is self-sufficient and self-transcendent is false. The argument to show the need for a Creator seems to resemble the Thomistic argument from efficient causality (to which the other four proofs are reducible). There is, however, a difference. In a static universe, I could not argue that the universe itself had a beginning, although I can see that things in it are finite and have beginnings or origins. For it is invalid to argue from the finitude and contingency of the part to the finitude and contingency of the whole. So, if the universe is static I could not tell whether as a whole it is finite or contingent. But if it grows, then it must have been born, and if born, then there must have been a Creator-Ground that gave it birth. With the empirical evidence of the universe evolving, it is possible to accept the Thomistic argument from finitude and contingency as recast in evolutionary categories.[5] Without the evolutionary category of birth, it would be impossible for us to argue that the universe had a Creator-Ground, for we would have to imagine process as a horizontal straight line that extends in either direction indefinitely and infinitely.

The Augustinian argument for God's reality, an argument basically followed by Anselm's ontological argument and Descartes' form of it, which starts from the rational self rather than from the external world, could likewise be recast in terms of evolutionary categories.

The mistake in the traditional idealistic argument is not the method of searching for God in reason. In fact, this is its greatest insight, because if God is to be found at all, he would most likely be found in the highest reality in the universe, namely, reason. In this reasoning, Augustine was more logical than Thomas who started from the cosmos. The mistake in the idealistic argument is precisely its idealism, as was pointed out by Thomas. However, what was a mistake to Thomas was not a mistake to the Platonist to whom the ideal was real. The Platonist saw reason as ideal, that is, as separated from the external world and from the body. Logically, he would discover God there, and he did not feel the need to make a transition from the ideal to the cosmological order, for the latter was seen as the region of sin, contingency and error, and hence quite irrelevant. God must be protected from it and should not be related to it. Making God relevant to the world was utter nonsense to a Platonist whose task it was to escape from this world. But for one for whom the world is real, the idealistic argument becomes irrelevant.

The recasting to be done is in our understanding of reason. Paradoxically, we believe the argument from reason would make God relevant to the world, not because reason is idealistic but precisely because it is the most immanent dimension of the evolving universe. Too long have we considered reason as ideal, as removed from the contingency of the world, as outside the evolutionary process. Teilhard makes a note of this false outlook:[6]

Looking at the progress of transformist views in the last hundred years, we are surprised to see how naïvely naturalists and physicists were able at the early stages to imagine themselves to be standing outside the universal stream they had just discovered. Almost incurably subject and object tend to become separated from each other in the act of knowing. We are continually inclined to isolate ourselves from the things and events which surround us, as though we were looking at them from outside, from the shelter of an observatory into which they were unable to enter, as though we were spectators, not elements, in what goes on.

Reason, however, is part of the evolutionary process, nay,

its most immanent part and paradoxically its most transcendent level since, being the future of the infrahuman level of evolution, it is the region of fullness of being and maturation, and hence the "within" of the becoming present and also its point of transcendence. With reason restored to its proper place in the world, we are not susceptible to the criticism of Thomas that we are making an illegitimate transition from the ideal to the real order.

Now, then, reason as part of the macrocosmic process is likewise in process, that is, it is still undergoing development as is manifested in the development of culture and civilization; the very constitution of history itself is the evolution of rational consciousness. In the previous chapter we also spoke of the evolution of reason toward the dimension of religious belief. If reason, then, is in process, it is subject to the universal law of growth, namely, that anything which grows needs a ground. Reason therefore requires a ground. This ground must be proportionate to the level of reason. Since reason is spiritual, personal, and hence fulfilled by love, then all these characteristics of reason must somehow be present in the Ground of reason, much as we would infer that the soil, in relation to the seed, is ultimately the source of its growth, flowering, and fruitfulness. Hence, the Ground of reason would be an attractive center of love, source of personalization and spiritual transformation.

Another merit of the traditional argument based on reason is the insight that God is somehow innate, somehow given *a priori* to reason. This insight is confirmed to be true by evolutionary analysis. In other words, the very posing of the question by reason, "Is there a God?" is a tautology, for the question contains the very answer. To see this, let us use again the example of the seed in relation to its ground. Thus, just as the very structure of the seed implies the existence of the ground and is intelligible only in relation to the ground, and *a fortiori* cannot even ask the question, "Is there a ground?" without implying the answer, so the very structure of reason, its very meaning and drive toward ultimate truth, implies the existence of God as Absolute Truth, as the very Ground of reason. Or again, just as the very existence of the plant implies its rootedness in the ground such that its very posing of the question, "Is there a ground?" would be tantamount to doubting its very existence, so the fact that I exist at all as a rational being already implies that God exists, as Descartes, for example, saw. Thus, reason implies in its very meaning the existence of its Ground, and the fact that it evolves at all implies the reality of its Ground. The whole process of evolution, as a matter of fact, tended toward reason in order that through it, the universe comes to an awareness of God as its Ground.

∾ God as Ground-Omega or Absolute Future

So far we have argued that if the universe is born, it must have a Creator-Ground, and if it grows, it must have a Ground of growth. Now we are going to argue that a universe that grows tends toward maturation, and that consequently it must have an Omega, that is, a convergent point in the absolute future.

We have to expect the universe to converge in the eschatological future; there has to be a critical threshold of radical transformation in which all the complexifying personal centers of consciousness are unified in an ultimate center of unity, if we are to be faithful to the mechanics and laws of the evolutionary process.

But what is the nature of this Omega? Is it other than the universe itself? It does not seem so at first glance, since the mature stage of a process is none other that the process itself. Thus, for example, the mature stage of a child, the adult, is none other than the same individual. If this is true, and we claim that the end of the maturation process is God, is this not tantamount to saying that the evolutionary process is really the evolution of God? As a matter of fact, some thinkers have identified God with the evolutionary process itself, seeing God as an emergent Deity.

To guide us in our reflection, it is necessary to consider examples of realities that are born, grow and mature. Perhaps an example taken from the level of noogenesis or the evolution of personal centers of consciousness would serve our need best, since the universe in its evolution has tended toward personalization and union in terms of love. Therefore, let us imagine the universe after the example of a human fetus in the womb which is therefore tending toward rebirth. This, incidentally, is the image used by St. Paul to convey the process of spiritual transformation and rebirth of the whole universe, in which Christ is the first-born or the first fruit. Pursuing the imagery, then, the implantation of the fertilized ovum in the womb would correspond to the birth of the universe, the development and self-differentiation of the ovum would be its growth, and the birth outside the womb would be its maturation. Now, the parents, in this instance, would at once be the *"creator"* of the ovum (that is, the conceivers), the *"ground"* of growth (at least, the mother), and the *"omega."*

That the parents are the "omega" or goal of the fetus may not be easy to see, since the term of the fetus is its full development. But let us consider, however, what is the full meaning of birth. Now, the birth of the fetus has for its purpose the self-revelation of the fetus to itself. In the womb, it could not know itself, for its consciousness is undeveloped; besides it does not have sufficiently developed sense organs to perceive itself and differentiate itself from others. Birth is a fuller stage of self-differentiation because the infant is now separated from the womb and thus is able to come to know itself as other. However, birth is but a stage in self-differentiation. To complete the process of self-revelation and self-differentiation, the infant must come to know its parents, not only as "other" but as the source of his identity. In knowing its parents, the child comes to know itself as the true image of his parents and the incarnation of their love. At a still deeper level of self-knowledge, the child needs to develop his personality. He must become a person. His personality, however, can be constituted only in terms of love. Consequently, the child needs the parents as the focus of his love and as the principle of integration of his personality. Therefore, the fetus does not merely tend toward its own maturation, but rather, in order to achieve maturation, in the fullest sense of the term, it has to have an "other," in this case, the parents, as point of convergence, as principle of unification and integration, as revealer to the child of what it is; and to the degree that the child learns to love with the aid of his parents, to that degree he is differentiated and thus revealed to himself for what he is.

Similarly, we need an Omega as Other to reveal the evolutionary process to itself, and in knowing itself, it can come to a full knowledge of itself as the image of the Other. God is the Absolute Future that attracts us by his love, and in drawing us to himself, we achieve maturation, self-differentiation and self-understanding. We need God to know our origin, to know the image in us, and to have a focus for our love, for it is in loving that we achieve differentiation at the deepest level of our beings. In scriptural language, God is he who is to come, just as the parents come before the child's view at birth. He is the Omega to whom we say: "Abba, Father!"

⌀ Conclusion

One of the reasons for the denial of the reality of God by modern secularizers, by Sartre, Nietzsche, Marx, etc., was the identification of God with the other-worldly, thus making God remote from the world and a threat to man's humanity because one had to abandon the world to attain God. But atheists should not now deny the reality of God on this score if God were presented as the Ground of the universe in process, since to attain the Ground is not a destruction of the universe or its abandonment, but its differentiation and fulfillment. God as Ground is not a threat to human growth or a threat to human and earthly values, for he is the necessary condition for their fruition and maturation. True humanization is a divinization, but this divinization is not at the expense of humanity, nor is it a going outside the world, for just as the more the seed sinks its roots in the ground, the more it becomes itself, so the more the universe unites itself with its Ground, the more it becomes fully itself.

These reflections here made may be considered as nothing but a commentary on the Apocalypse: "I am the Alpha and the Omega, the beginning and the end, says the Lord God, who is and who was and who is coming, the Almighty" (1:8). Thus, God who gives "birth" to the universe, or God as Creator-Ground, is the Alpha or he-who-was; God as Ground of evolution or growth is God as he-who-is; and God as the Absolute Future of the universe, the term of the process, is the Omega, or he-who-is-coming, or will be.

4

ETERNITY AS
THE FULLNESS
OF TIME

I n the last chapter we made an
attempt to formulate the notion
of God in terms of this-worldly
categories, by seeing him as the Creator-Ground, the Ground
of Growth, and the Ground-Omega. But we cannot hold on
to these immanentistic categories while at the same time
thinking of God's eternity as the absence of time. For eternity's timelessness implies that God is not really in time and
history.

Many efforts at situating God in time and history have
been made. Ogden summarizes some of these.[1] Bonhoeffer
speaks of the God of a secular faith, of a "suffering" God,[2]
a God who is radically different from the Absolute God of
classic theism, but Bonhoeffer's God requires conceptual clarification that he does not furnish. Tillich presents us with a
God that tries to go beyond naturalism and supernaturalism
by showing God as "self-transcendent" and as the ground of
being of whatever exists.[3] But Tillich is still very much

bound by the categories of classical metaphysics, especially that of "being." Ogden, while paying tribute to the constructive efforts of Bultmann, Bonhoeffer and Tillich in the fight against supernaturalism, nevertheless notes a fundamental weakness in them, namely, that "the conceptuality these theologians employ is insufficiently developed, so that what they mean when they speak of God is left obscure or uncertain or else their conception of God is still determined by the same metaphysical-theological premises by which the supernaturalism they seek to transcend is itself determined." [4]

With regard to the efforts of the death-of-God theologians, Ogden observes that to base Christian theology on the secularistic premise that God is dead is to make an assessment of our cultural situation that is "completely undiscriminating in simply assuming that secularism is an essentially unified and internally consistent outlook." [5] And while the attempts of the existential-phenomenological tradition in formulating the notion of God in terms of the historical and interpersonal do, to a certain extent, describe God's presence in history, the result is often quite unreliable because it is overly subjectivistic, and hence unverifiable.

Ogden's own view is to look upon God as Process, as a social reality that interacts with human persons in a relational way, and who is temporal and historical because he grows, matures, evolves and becomes, while at the same time being God because he is likewise infinite, eternal, unchanging and immutable.

An extreme view of God as Process is the Hegelian view which identifies God with history itself. The divine will is manifested through the laws of the state and through the great heroes that consciously or unconsciously carry it out. As a criticism of this view we might ask what evidence we have that God is history. Is this not an *a prioristic* interpretation of history? And is it not at the expense of human values, human freedom, in short, of man himself? As a reaction to the Hegelian view, the Marxistic view takes the other extreme by saying that all history is human history.[7]

Leslie Dewart[8] criticizes both the Hegelian and Marxistic views of history in terms of his theory of the development of truth by saying that to reduce history to man or to reduce it to God would be nothing else but the self-actualization of an original potentiality: matter in the first case, Absolute Spirit in the second. But neither view is evolutionary; there is really no creativity and novelty. Dewart's view is that "God does not dip his finger into history; he totally immerses himself in it."[9] God's "temporality consists in being *present to history*. The fundamental relation between man and God is found in the reality of history. It consists in the mutual presence of God and man in the conscious creation of the world."[10] Again, Dewart says, "God is temporal in the same way that man is, namely, in the sense that he makes time. On the other hand, since God is not a being, his temporality does not create him. Unlike man, as he makes time God does not make himself; what he makes is being."[11] These are the "suggestions" that Dewart makes to dehellenize the eternity of God.[12]

The path we are going to follow here in secularizing eternity is the one indicated in my first book[13] which is based on the philosophy of process I have outlined.

The first step we are going to take to secularize eternity is to reflect on the historical basis for the view that eternity is timelessness. It would seem that there is no essential similarity at all between time and eternity since there is a chasm between God and creation. As Rudolf Otto so well observes, God is the wholly Other.[14] But the paradox is that there has to be a similarity between them because *omne agens agit sibi simili*. In other words, if God created time, then time must somehow be in God. The traditional answer to the relation between time and eternity is that time is in God but not univocally as in creatures. It is claimed that just as all creaturely perfections are in God *eminenter* (in a more perfect way), so time is in God in a more perfect way. But what, precisely, is this more perfect way is not explained. Instead, it is confidently asserted that there is a similarity between time and eternity by virtue of the analogy of being. One wonders, however, whether there is any basis at all for the analogy if eternity is viewed as the complete absence of time. There would rather be total dissimilarity. If this is so, it is difficult to see how a timeless God can relate himself to the temporal. How can God be truly immanent in all things that evolve if his eternity situates him outside time? How can he be Lord of Time if he is not within time to control it? If he cannot know temporal human existence with all its cares and anxieties, how can he be truly compassionate and merciful?

On the part of man, if man's goal is a participation in God, then to be with God is to participate in his eternity, but since eternity is timelessness, this implies a withdrawal from time. Now, for the medieval man for whom time was negative or at least neutral, there was neither theoretical difficulty nor spiritual tension in accepting this dialectic of withdrawal. But the modern Christian who sees time as creative, positive and humanizing finds the dialectic of withdrawal from time quite absurd, to say the least.

As long as we hold on to the traditional view of God's eternity as timelessness, it is impossible, I believe, not only to show God's immanence in time and history, but also to convince others that Christianity truly values the temporal and the secular.

What I would like to offer as a tentative solution, a solution that I offer here for comment and criticism, is to see God's eternity, not as the absence of time, but as the Fullness of Time.

However, no sooner do we propose this notion than objections arise. For is not to speak of God's eternity as the Fullness of Time tantamount to saying that God is the fullness of contingency and of change, and to denying that God is the Immutable, the Unchanging? Is it not to identify God with Matter to call his eternity the Fullness of Time? And since matter is the highest form of contingency, transiency, and mutability, would not God then be equated with pure potency? And how could God be temporal like material creation? Is this not to destroy God's transcendence and his Otherness and to land us into pantheism?

The objections are well made; consequently, we must accept as a necessary condition of a valid formulation of God's eternity that it save and show God's Otherness from creatures. However, the point I wish to make is that I do not think that God's eternity must necessarily be seen as an absence of time to save the Otherness of God. The real crux of the matter is whether contingency is of the essence of time or not. For if contingency were essential, then to say that God is the Fullness of Time is also to say that he is the fullness of contingency.

The first step in our reflection is a reexamination of the Greek notion of time in order to get a better understanding of the right direction we should follow.

Greek thought saw time as essentially contingent in character. Time for Plato was unreal. By this he meant that it was not permanent like the immutable eternal forms in the otherworldly realm. Time is but the moving imitation of eternity.[15] Things in time are impermanent because they are mere shadows and copies of the unchanging ideas. Plotinus elaborates on his master, Plato. Time, says Plotinus, is the measure of degradation which resulted from the fall of the sensible world from the One.[16] The farther one went into the future, the greater the degradation. Time therefore as it moves into the future is negative. Where Plato merely observed the shadowy nature of time, Plotinus emphasized its destructive or negative nature. Aristotle also saw the destructive nature of time. For him time is the measure of motion which of its very nature is an undoing. As Aristotle says: "It is in time that all is engendered and destroyed. . . . One can see that time itself is the cause of destruction rather than generation. . . . For change itself is an undoing; it is only by accident a cause of generation and existence." [17] Again he says: "For we are wont to say that time wears, that all things age in time, all is erased by time, but never that we have learnt or that we have grown young and handsome; for time in itself is more truly a cause of destruction, since time is the number of movement, and movement undoes that which is." [18]

With this view of time as contingent and negative, God's eternity could not be equated with time or have anything to do with time. In fact, as Louis Bouyer observes, "in Greek thought, eternity and time cannot possibly be reconciled. The two notions can be said to characterize two universes parallel to one another. Eternity is a characteristic not only of immutable, but of purely ideal realities. Time belongs exclusively to the world of matter and of change." [19] Oscar Cullmann also makes the same observation:

For Greek thinking in its Platonic formulation there exists between time and eternity a qualitative difference, which is not completely expressed by speaking of a distinction between limited and unlimited duration of time. For Plato, eternity is not endlessly extended time, but something quite different; it is timelessness. Time in Plato's view is only the *copy* of eternity thus understood.[20]

It was Plato who taught us to contrast time and eternity, although such an antithesis is alien to biblical thought.[21] The result is that our spirituality has been infected with the Greek dichotomy between time and eternity. For the Greeks, the idea that

> redemption is to take place through divine action in the course of events in time is impossible. Redemption in hellenism can consist only in the fact that we are transferred from existence in this world, an existence bound to the circular course of time, into that Beyond which is removed from time and is already and always available. The Greek conception of blessedness is thus spatial; it is determined by the contrast between this world and the timeless Beyond; it is not a time conception determined by the opposition between Now and Then.[22]

The Greek view of time and eternity has come down even to our day. As Cullmann observes "far and wide the Christian Church and Christian theology distinguish time and eternity in the Platonic-Greek manner." [23]

Yet, in the Scriptures, God is closer to time than to timelessness. Time is a sacred category in salvation history, for it is in the *Kairos* or sacred time that God is present. In fact, in the New Testament, the divine epiphany in Christ is represented in terms of temporal categories: his incarnation or birth, his life, passion, death and rebirth or resurrection. And Christ himself is seen as God's supreme *Kairos* or fullness of time. But with the Greek view of time as contingent and destructive, the early theologians who had to preach the faith to the

Greeks could not very well speak of God as the Fullness of Time. Since for the Greeks the timeless was better than the temporal, God's eternity had to be shown as timelessness. God had to be separated as far as possible from time, his abode represented as a heaven beyond this earth. He is allowed occasional forays into history, first in the instantaneous or non-temporal act of creation, and second in the physical pre-motion or concursus he gives for activities of secondary causes. But today, we are no longer in the Greek context. Time is no longer destructive but positive. It is incumbent on the Christian philosopher and theologian to reflect whether they should go on teaching that God's eternity is timelessness.

As a result of biblical research we now realize that the Scriptures speak of God's eternity in terms of time, not time-lessness. Eternity is the time of God, which time is contrasted from our time:

> The eternity of God is first manifested in the fact that he was and acted before all things and all life: before the individual life (Jer 1:5), before the people of Israel, before the created world (Ps 90:2). Likewise he is the one who will be after all created existence. He is the "Alpha and the Omega, the beginning and the end" (Rev 21:6; cf. 22:13). His divine time overflows, holds together, and envelops all other times. . . . The eternal life of God does not of course cease to have its specific dimension within the period between the creation and the last judgment, God is "he who is and who was and who is to come" (Rev 1:4; 4:8).[24]

Thus, God's eternity is not so much timelessness as the Fullness of Time, for to speak of God as "he who is and who was and who is to come" implies time, not timelessness. Cullmann notes that primitive Christianity understood God's eternity in terms of time:

Primitive Christianity knows nothing of a timeless God. The "eternal" God is he who was in the beginning, is now, and will be in all the future, "who is, who was, and who will be" (Rev. 1:4). Accordingly, his eternity can and must be expressed in this "naive" way, in terms of endless time.[25]

Thus, the Scriptures settle the question of the method of expressing God's eternity in favor of the category of the temporal instead of the timeless. But this is not the end of the matter for us moderns; it is the beginning of theological reflection. How is God's eternity to be expressed in terms of time? Must we accept that in God there is contingency? That he becomes? Some secularizers, accepting the view that time is of its essence contingent, logically predicate contingency of God's eternity. Thus, God grows, becomes, evolves.

I am not ready to accept the view that God evolves because of my concern to safeguard what I believe is also quite biblical about God's eternity, namely, its immutability. For God's time remains the same "yesterday and today and forever" (Heb 13:8).[26] God is "not affected by the vicissitudes which mark the time of his creatures, for on the contrary he remains the absolute master of time: 'With the Lord one day is as a thousand years and a thousand years as one day' (2 Pet 3:8; cf. Ps 90:4)." [27]

The presupposition in the position that if God is temporal, then he becomes and grows, is that time of its very nature is contingent. It is this contingency of time that I wish to question. I believe that along with the Greek notion of eternity, the hellenic notion of time as contingent should also be dehellenized. For as Gerhard Von Rad observes:

The attitude of Western man to linear time is, generally speaking, naive; time is seen as an infinitely long straight line on which the individual can mark such past and future events as he can ascertain. This time-span has a midpoint, which is our own present day. From it the past stretches back and the future forward. But today one of the few things of which we can be quite sure is that this concept of absolute time, independent of events, and, like the blanks of a questionnaire, only needing to be filled up with data which will give it content, was unknown to Israel.[28]

I believe that it is wrong to take this linear notion of time and apply it to God's eternity, even if we make qualifications. If the Israelites had this view of time, then I do not think that they would have expressed God's eternity in terms of the category of time.

It is within the context of an evolutionary view of time that I shall attempt to get a proper understanding of God's time, first because our general purpose is to make God's eternity relevant to our modern evolutionary world, and second because this seems to be the context in which the Scriptures thought of God's time. I do not mean thay they had a knowledge of scientific evolution but that they looked upon reality as a process of growth. Thus, according to the *Vocabulary of the Bible,* "just as the seed cast into the earth leads naturally to the full blossoming of the plant, so the work of God in the world holds within itself the promise of its fulfillment. Growth is characteristic of the work of God; it develops progressively from the imperfect to the perfect, from the inception to the completion."[29] Again: "The kingdom of heaven has taken root in the world, where it was sown as a tiny seed" (Mt 13:31-33, 44).[30]

My reflections on the nature of evolutionary time show that it is not essentially contingent and that it is possible to speak of God's eternity as the Fullness of Time without implying that God becomes or is contingent. Let me proceed to argue the point, first by a theoretical analysis of the nature of evolutionary time, contrasting it with the hellenic view of time, and second by a confirmation and verification of this analysis of evolutionary time as noncontingent and immanent by observing the actual process of evolution itself.

The view that time is essentially contingent is an untenable position if we accept the evolutionary law applicable to all things that evolve, namely, that a thing is not what it is, but what it shall be—or as Teilhard expressed it, all growing magnitudes in the world must become different so as to remain themselves.[31]

In order to know in a negative way, at least, what time shall be, we must know what time is now. Obviously, time now is historical; it is also contingent. Everybody would agree with this observation. But I also presuppose that time now is evolutionary, that is, that it is tending toward maturation. This presupposition allows me to conclude that if time now is contingent, then at its maturation it would be non-contingent. If time remains contingent at the end as at the beginning, then there was really no evolutionary change. But my presupposition precisely is that time is evolutionary. If we accept this presupposition, then time cannot remain the same. It must change qualitatively, from contingency to non-contingency. This conclusion, of course, jolts us. How can this be? Such an assertion implies that time is destroyed, that there is no longer any time. But this is not evolution. The conclusion jolts us because we have identified the essence of time with contingency. So long has been the tradition behind the notion of time's contingency that it has acquired the strength of an absolute truth. And even today when we have pretty much accepted evolution as universal, we still, unconsciously perhaps, exclude time from this universal law. But why? Why should not time itself evolve? Why must it forever be contingent? Is this not to look at time statically? We allow an oak to evolve from an acorn to a non-acorn (full grown oak), a non-living reality (matter) to evolve to the living, the non-sensitive (vegetative) to evolve to the sensitive, the sensitive to evolve toward the suprasensitive or self-conscious, and so on. We are able to see continuity in them, yet we do not allow time to evolve from contingency to non-contingency or from transiency to immanence.

The reason for our failure to see that time could evolve from contingency to non-contingency without being destroyed is perhaps due to the popular image we have of time as a straight line that goes on and on. With this view of time, the only type of change that would not destroy the nature of time would be for time to go on flowing interminably into the future. An evolution of time would be interpreted as a variation in the speed of the motion or perhaps in its direction. Given this view of time, a change that implied the cessation of con-tingency or of becoming would not be an evolution of time, obviously, but its destruction.

Regarding the popular view of time as a straight line stretch-ing backward and forward, it should be observed that it is not only naive as Von Rad has mentioned,[32] but also quite unreal and non-evolutionary. In other words, this popular view of time, paradoxically enough, is static. This statement again surprises us, for how can any view of time be described as static? The eternal as timeless is static, yes, but not time. In reply, let me observe that I am not using the term static and its correlative, dynamic, within the hellenic pattern of thought which applies the former to eternity and the latter to time. I am using the terms in an evolutionary context. Thus, within the evolutionary context, there is such a thing as a static view of time and a dynamic view. Let me explain what I mean, using the acorn as an illustration. Now, if the acorn were to go on growing in size without ever changing into an oak, but simply becoming bigger and bigger, all the while retaining its form as an acorn, then, the change of the original ordinary-sized acorn into a super-acorn is a change that should be properly called static, in order to contrast it with the real change in which the acorn qualitatively evolves into a non-acorn, i.e., into an oak. Where the original form remains the same throughout the change, then this change which is purely quantitative is considered static, as opposed to the other in which there is a change of form and which therefore is properly called dynamic or evolutionary. Similarly, a view of time that goes on and on without change of form is a static and naive view. The kind of time I am talking about is evolutionary.

Evolutionary time is not a succession of moments, each of which appears for a flitting instant and is lost forever. In evolutionary time, nothing is lost. The past is carried over into the present, so that it is false to imagine the present like a bead in a string of beads, or a drop from a dripping faucet, each bead or drop having equal value and weight as the others. No, the present is heavy with the past and is of greater ontological weight than the past, so that we can justly say that the present is fuller time than the past. And as the present tends toward the future, it attains the fullness of time. However, we must hasten to add that the fullness of time is not merely the quantitative sum of previous times, for this, too, would be no more than the case of an acorn becoming a super-acorn, or a bucket being filled by drops from the faucet. Rather, when the fullness of time is reached, there is a qualitative transformation, as in the case of the acorn becoming an oak, or water brought to boiling point becoming vapor, or instinct becoming reflection, or molecular increase becoming cellular.

The foregoing cases in which quantitative change evolved toward the qualitative are examples of evolutionary time.

Now, what I would like to show is that evolutionary time evolves from the contingent to the non-contingent. This is a step to showing that to speak of God's eternity as the Fullness of Time is not to imply contingency.

To observe evolutionary time, it must not be seen as a container in which things that evolve are contained, for such a view of time is still basically hellenic; much less should it be considered as a succession of moments tending toward its term because this is non-evolutionary. Evolutionary time is one with the things that evolve, so it is the things themselves that must be observed, but from the point of view of a thing's ability to possess and to gather time. For example, man as a given stage of the evolutionary process is able to gather the past, present and even part of the future in his consciousness. But let us start from the beginning in order to see the development of time from contingency to non-contingency, from transiency to immanence.

First, a brief definition of contingency and transiency, and their correlates non-contingency and immanence, is in order. Contingent time would be one that is chaotic, without direction, short-lived, unstable, whereas a non-contingent time is one that is ordered, directed and able to maintain itself for longer periods. Transient time is one that flows out, whereas immanent time is one that is able to get hold of itself, collect and possess itself; hence, it is present to itself or becomes interior to itself.

We observe that at the lowest level of the evolutionary process, time is contingent in the sense that electronic and atomic radiations are short-lived, measured in millionths of a second; the movement is chaotic, diffused, haphazard, indeterminate as shown in the cloud chamber or the Brownian movement of molecules; the time is transient because entropy takes over; the movements are lost instead of being collected in the thing and perfective of the thing.

As we go higher up, however, the entropy is counteracted by a higher form of movement—life. Compared to the physical, transient random and fragile motions of the atoms and molecules, life is directed, better organized, longer-lived, more stable and immanent.[33] As Teilhard notes there is an advance in interiority,[34] and with this advance, time comes to a greater possession of itself. Where before, time was confined to the atomic and molecular zone, now it is possessed of a new dimension, the biosphere. This new space-time dimension not only contains itself but also the past history of cosmogenesis. Time evolved toward the cell, therefore, in order that entropy which is the flowing out of time and energy through chemical disintegration might be counteracted by cell reproduction so that time is able to prolong itself without crumbling.[35] Through the association of one cell with another, cells build themselves in sufficient bulk so as to be able to "escape innumerable external obstacles (capillary attraction, osmotic pressure, chemical variation of the medium, etc.) which paralyze the microscopic organism."[36] Through association also, the organism "is able to find room inside itself to lodge the countless mechanisms added successively in the course of its differentiation."[37] Thus time does not flow out.

But the story of life itself as a higher manifestation of the evolution of time, though non-contingent and immanent compared to the lower stages of time, is, in terms of the higher stage of consciousness, quite contingent and unstable. For the story of the evolution of life is the story of innumerable chances, fumbling and gropings through countless ages.[38] "Life advances by mass effects, by dint of multitudes flung into action without apparent plan. Milliards of germs and millions of adult growths jostling, shoving, and devouring one another, fight for elbow room and for the best and largest living space."[39]

Time manifested as life multiplies itself in countless individuals, species, genera, phyla, etc., in order to prolong itself, for it can maintain itself only by differentiating itself. The purpose of time is to conquer itself, that is, prevent any part of itself flowing out. So from one zoological group to another, time marched on in search of itself, by trying to be transparent to itself. In the phenomenon of memory, time is able to attain an inchoate form of reduplication, and thus for the first time can really be said to grasp part of itself. Where before in the unconscious level, time was gathered without being consciously grasped, now there is a conscious gathering of time, so that the past is able to coexist with the present reduplicatively. In the effort to attain full reduplication. memory multiplied in various individuals, but even this movement of memory is one-sided, or unidirectional. In order to fulfill itself, memory had to double itself by tending to the other direction—forward—and in the process a new space-time dimension was born, the noosphere, in which the future is attained by the foresight of reason.

In man, time has become human temporality, human history. Compared to the infrahuman level's space-time dimension, human time is able to gather the past, the present and to a degree the future. In man, the past (pre-history and history) is gathered, not only because man is the product of the previous stages of the process, but also because he is able to attain it consciously through his memory. And through reflection, what is gathered by memory is able to coexist with the present, while through foresight, imagination, hope and belief, past and present are able to coexist with the future. Through human consciousness, then, time for the first time becomes consciously purposive, and hence non-contingent; time becomes transparent to itself, interior to itself, and hence immanent. Human temporality represents the fullness of time of the infrahuman space-time dimensions; toward it they tended as to their eschatological future or "eternity" in order to be.

At this point in our analysis we can fairly well establish that evolutionary time evolved from contingency to non-contingency, from transiency to immanence. However, we have not yet attained a true concept of the fullness of time because the non-contingency of human temporality is a relative one. Therefore let us consider the evolution of human temporality to see whether we could attain a true concept of the fullness of time that could serve as the basis for a concept of God's eternity as the Fullness of Time.

Human temporality, though immanent and non-contingent relative to the infrahuman levels, is still open toward the future. Because the dimension of the future, not only of present history but of the eschatological future, is not yet attained, human temporality does not possess the fullness of time. This lack of fullness of time is manifested in existential stages of insecurity, feelings of anxiety and fear about an uncertain future which it does not know and possess. In the effort to attain security and non-contingency, human temporality harks back to the past in an infantile way, dwelling on past accomplishments, or it busies itself with the affairs of the present. But true security is not to be found in time past or present but in future time. Human temporality therefore tries to divine what the future may bring; it takes the whole of itself (past, present and its future) and puts its whole destiny in an Absolute (ideology, deity, even the self) in the hope and belief that it may be reborn to a new space-time dimension, the eschatological, and thus possess the fullness of time.

What is the fullness of time that human temporality is searching for? This fullness of time coincides with the fullness of growth and maturation of humanity. Now, the meaning of the fullness of growth with respect to a given process is that the end is reached, there is no more becoming—hence, the cessation of contingency. But we have to be careful in imagining properly what the cessation of becoming implies, for we could fall into the mistake of imagining it as the cessation of all movement, much like a moving line that suddenly comes to a stop. As we said earlier, this would not be the perfection of time but its destruction. The cessation of becoming which coincides with the fullness of growth implies the beginning of fullest activity, for when growth is finished, it also means the full possession and maturation of one's powers. The fullness of growth as the cessation of becoming should be imagined after the example of a child that becomes an adult. The child is contingent in many ways—its activity is not fully directed; it makes many mistakes; it also means that it may not reach adulthood. But the adult, relative to the child, is non-contingent—that is, he has reached the fullness of growth, there is no longer any growing, for an adult *qua* adult does not become what he already is. Becoming in this case terminates in being; however, being must not be understood as the absence of activity, but rather the fullness of it.

There is the common but false impression that becoming is more dynamic than being. This is true when becoming is identified with temporality and change, while being is identified as in the case of Plato with the pure and immutable forms which are beyond time, or with essence, as in the case of Aristotle, which is secure from time and history. Because of this inherited context, come theists, in the effort to attain a dynamic concept of God, logically predicate becoming of him. For the only other alternative in the hellenic context is non-becoming or timelessness. To achieve dynamism in God, however, a great price is paid—that of admitting becoming in God. Those who do not admit becoming in God are justly accused of having a static notion of God. But this accusation is valid as long as it is a discussion between theists of the hellenic tradition. What is forgotten, however, is that the hellenic context is not an absolute context. It is not necessarily the case that to deny becoming in God is to have a static notion of God. In the evolutionary context, being is more dynamic than becoming, for it coincides with the fullness of growth which means the fullness of activity, whereas becoming which implies the incompleteness of growth naturally lacks the fullness of activity. Paradoxically then, a becoming God is not as dynamic as a "non-becoming" God within the evolutionary context.

So far, we have analyzed the notion of the fullness of time as implying the fullness of being, of activity and the absence of contingency. But the notion needs further clarification before we can speak of God's time as the Fullness of Time. For the fullness of time we have analyzed is the result of growth. To apply this notion to God would imply that God emerged, that he was born and matured.

It is necessary to distinguish the fullness of time of the universe which is the result of evolution and maturation from the Fullness of Time of God which is the source of evolutionary time. Perhaps the use of scriptural examples will help us see the distinction. Thus the Scriptures speak of God as the source of growth. The work of God is seen as a seed which evolves toward maturation [40] or as a tiny seed that takes root (Mt 13:31-33, 34). Again, Israel is seen in relation to God as a child, born of Yahweh, nurtured by him, etc. Therefore, guided by these examples, we can consider God metaphorically as Ground or as Womb and the universe as the seed or the fetus.

In the examples proposed, we can distinguish two senses of the term "fullness of time." Thus, there is the fullness of time of the fetus or the seed, and the fullness of time of the mother (womb) or of the ground. The fullness of time of the seed or of the fetus is apparent, for they are in process of growth.

But it is not quite easy to see how the mother or the ground can be said to possess the fullness of time since they are not growing or becoming. But consider that without the mother or the ground, the fetus or the seed would not have any time in it. In other words, a seed left alone and apart from the ground has no time because it does not become; it does not possess its future; it does not even have its present. Nor can it give time to itself, since it is not its own ground. It is the ground that gives time to the seed. Again, a non-viable fetus apart from the womb is a dead fetus, and what is dead, obviously, has no time. It is the womb that gives time to the fetus. Thus, we can see that the womb or the ground can be said to be the fullness of time. They are the fullness of time in relation to the fetus or the seed in three ways: (1) as source of initial time by giving initial becoming or life to the seed or fetus; (2) as source of continued time or growth; and (3) as source of maturation—hence, of fullness of time and growth of the seed or fetus.

With the analogy proposed, it is possible to understand in some way, at least, how God can be said to be the Fullness of Time. Thus, God as Creator-Ground is the source of the initial time of the universe; as Ground of growth, he is the source of present time; and as Ground-Omega, he is the source of maturation or fullness of time. Our analysis of God's eternity as the Fullness of Time seems to be confirmed by the Scriptures. Thus, God's time is seen as overflowing, holding together and enveloping all other times.[41] The imagery of God as Ground or as Womb explains how our time, which is like that of the growing seed or fetus, is enveloped or held together or suffused by God's Time. God, as the source of time in the three ways we explained it, seems to conform to the scriptural view of God's time as "he who was and who is and who is to come" (Rev 1:4; 4:8). Thus, God as source of past time is he who was, of present time as he who is, and of future or eschatological time as he who is to come.

But do not the classic and medieval formulations of God speak of him also as Creator, as Preserver (*creatio continuata*) and as Final Cause or End? That God is Creator and End of creation is a common datum of all formulations of the faith. However, the way this is explained is another thing. And here difficulty arises for the traditional formulation, since if God's eternity is seen as the absence of time, it is difficult, to say the least, to see how he could possibly be the source of time. In fact, with a view of time as negative, as source of mutability and contingency, some other way has to be found to explain time's origin in order to safeguard God's causality, by saying, e.g., that time is the measure of the degradation resulting from the fall, or that God created a metaphysical and finished universe through an instantaneous creation in which every species was present from the beginning, instead of a world of becoming and growth.

If God who created time also said that it was good, then a formulation of God's eternity must show it to be the source of time, just as the traditional formulation of God as Perfect Good, Absolute Truth and Supreme Being clearly show God to be the source of all good, truth and being. Yet, eternity as the absence of time can in no way show how it is the source of time or how it is relevant to history at all. Furthermore, if time is good, it is difficult to see why we should be withdrawing from it and hankering for the timeless instead. These difficulties were not present in the Middle Ages because time was seen negatively so that life became an escape from time. But today, with our awareness of the positive value of time, tension is produced by the old formulation of eternity as the absence of time. To resolve the tension, God should no longer be seen as *Actus Purus*, timeless, a mere preserver of a finished universe, nor should Exodus 3:14 be pressed into the service of this static outlook to mean that God is he who is, that is, timeless existence. Rather, God should be seen in a dynamic way, as source of growth, as evolver of the evolving universe. Hence, for God to create is the same as for him to evolve, to mature, to unite to himself; evolution is God's creative action expressed in time. And Exodus 3:14 should be interpreted in the light of the Apocalypse, for St. John purposely wrote this work as the fullness and recapitulation of the first book, Genesis, in which the first creation and the first earth are recapitulated and fulfilled in the New Creation and the New Earth, and the apocalyptic woman with child recapitulates the woman and child of Genesis. So, the "I will be who I will be" of Exodus is recapitulated in the Apocalypse as, "I am the Alpha and the Omega, the beginning and the end, says the Lord God, who is and who was and who is coming" (1:8). Thus, God as Absolute Future contains all time; he is the Lord and Fullness of Time. If the traditional formulations of God show him to be the Perfect Good, Absolute Truth and Supreme Being, since goodness, truth and being are positive values, then there should not be too great a difficulty in accepting a formulation of God's eternity as Absolute or Perfect Time, since time is now revealed to us as positive, thanks to the discovery of evolution.

There should be no fear that, in speaking of God's eternity as the Fullness of Time, we imply that he is contingent, that he becomes or evolves. For God's Fullness of Time is like the fullness of time of the mother in relation to the child, or of the ground in relation to the seed. Thus, the mother does not grow or develop; the child does. Nor does the ground grow; the seed does. Similarly, though God is the Fullness of Time, he does not grow or become. It is when we begin to think abstractly and conceptually about God's time that it becomes illogical to suppose that God does not become or evolve, or when we apply an unphilosophical view of time to the under-

standing of the notion of the Fullness of Time that we fall
into all sorts of difficulties. There is no dogma or self-evident
philosophic principle that says that time is essentially contingent, that becoming is more dynamic than being, defined as
the fullness of growth and therefore of activity.

◈ Conclusion

What has the reformulation of God's eternity as the Fullness of Time gained for us? First of all, it produces a revolution in our Christian thinking. No longer need we represent
the Christian life as a movement from time to timelessness,
but quite the reverse—from timelessness to time. We are thus
able to align our theology with the scientific and philosophic
disciplines which already have made the conversion to the
modern dynamic world-view from the classic static world-
view—hence from the Ptolemaic to the Copernican, from the
Aristotelian eternal species to the Darwinian evolution of
species, from the metaphysical to the temporal or historical
and evolutionary in philosophy and theology. In this specific
case, the conversion must be from *Theos* as timeless to *Theos*
as the Fullness of Time. God as the central category of
theology, if thus temporalized, would require a restructuring
of the other parts of theology.

If God is the Fullness of Time, then we have to accustom
ourselves to seeing that our present time is not already time;
rather, it is lack of time. Also, we have to accustom ourselves to seeing that to go beyond our time is not to go to the
timeless, but toward the fullness of time. The conditioning of
centuries of the static view, aided by our common-sense view
of things, prevents us from being truly philosophical, that

is, seeing beyond appearances which lead us astray into believing that time is already time. If time were already time,
then it would not evolve. But if we accept time's evolution,
then it is not yet fully itself; it lacks itself. Our time is a lack of
time, which, in relation to God's Fullness of Time, is timelessness. Ironically, the timelessness that we attributed to God
is really a projection of our infantile state of timelessness,
and is an indication of the infantile state of our traditional
theologies which see God's eternity as timelessness.

Second, in terms of Christian practice, if God is the Fullness of Time, I find it possible now to explain to myself and
to others why Christianity is not other-worldly. I no longer
have to represent my going to God as a departure from time
and history.[42] In fact, to attain God as the Absolute Future
who is also the Fullness of Time, I must perforce be occupied
with the present and the tasks of the present, for it is only
in and through the present that I can advance into the future.
The Christian life is an incarnation in time, but this time is
not ceaseless becoming; it is evolutionary, tending toward
eschatological time. Hence, to be incarnational is to be eschatological and vice versa.

If God's eternity were seen as the Fullness of Time, I can
somehow understand how God is immanent in history and
in my human temporality. God is the very source of my
temporality, the Ground of my growth, and the fullness of it.
I am thus able to reconcile my view of God with the modern
view of man as his historicity.

That particularly vexing problem, whether to go to God is
not to abandon the world, seems to find resolution here too.
The difficulty for most Christians is caused by two false
assumptions: (1) that the world is already itself, that is,
finished, and (2) that God's eternity is timelessness. We have
to deny both to find a solution to our problem. We have to
see that the world is evolving and that perfection is in the

possession of the fullness of time. Consequently, for the world to tend to God is not for it to be other-worldly, but to be fully itself, since God is the source of its maturation. The world does not abandon time, because in attaining God, it attains the fullness of its own time. With God's eternity as the Fullness of Time, it is possible now to bring back to our awareness the scriptural teaching, ignored by traditional theology, that the whole world is going to be redeemed. In the traditional view of God's eternity as timelessness, enormous difficulty is created in explaining how essentially temporal things like the world and the body can participate in God's timelessness without their ultimate destruction. As a consequence, the old theology deemphasized or conveniently ignored the fact of the resurrection of the body and the redemption of material creation and spoke instead and almost exclusively of the salvation of the soul pictured as being supratemporal and metaphysical.

With God's eternity shown as the Fullness of Time, Christian humanism becomes a true acceptance of the temporal. Christians can cooperate with the Marxists in transforming the world, for we are both interested in attaining the fullness of time for the world. The only difference in our outlooks is that we Christians expect the epiphany of God in the end; for the Marxists, there is only the epiphany of man.

5

THE ABSENCE
OF GOD AND
GOD-LANGUAGE

Theists are agreed on the reality of God; however, not all are agreed on the way God's reality is to be explained. I am not speaking here of so-called "proofs" for God's existence, for as I have indicated earlier, I do not believe in natural theology. Rather, I am speaking of the way one's belief in God is to be elaborated. Now, in traditional elaborations and thinking about the reality of God, the basic presupposition has been that to accept the reality of God is also to accept his presence. As a consequence, to show the reality of God is the same as to show his presence. I would like to dissent from this basic method, for it does not necessarily follow that to accept the reality of God is to imply his presence. An absent God is not any less real than a present one.

It is difficult enough to show God's reality, but it is made more difficult, I think, because of the failure to distinguish between two senses of the term "presence." In the first sense, presence is opposed to non-being or non-existence; in the second sense, presence is opposed to spatial or temporal absence. Presence in the first sense is opposed to total absence or absolute nothingness, while in the second sense, it is opposed to partial or provisional absence of a present reality. Because this distinction was not always made, many of those who tried to show the reality of God also tried to show his actual presence here and now, that is, that he is "spatially" and temporally present in the present, meeting enormous difficulties in the attempt. Thus, as one writer has observed, "the debate about God takes the form of a quest for data about God and experience of God." [1] The same writer observes that this manner of asking the question was influenced by the scientific method of searching for scientific data. In the particular problem of God, the quest accordingly took the form of looking for the answer to the question, "What is that area of human experiencing in which awareness of God is to be found?" [2] Various answers were proposed: Schleiermacher tried to base the presence of God in feelings of absolute dependence, Barth in direct revelation from God, Bultmann in existential experience of pure inwardness, Thomism in the analogy of being which leads to the awareness of Supreme Being, Tillich in asking the right questions about ultimate concern.[3]

It is not only traditional theologies that try to show the reality of God by way of his presence. It has always been the desire of many people throughout the centuries to wish "to 'experience' God or at least to search for a God who would speak in their lives." [4] This desire to look for the presence of God is not only an ancient and medieval problem but is the search of millions of people today.[5]

Even many secularizers attempt to show God's presence in time and history. But I believe that all attempts to make God appear is bound to fail. If one claims that God is present, then the linguistic analysts have a field day in showing the illogicality of the affirmation. For if we are using time and history in the accepted senses of the term, we would be forced to produce an historical or empirical evidence of God, which obviously we cannot. On the other hand, if we say we are using the term historical or temporal in another sense, we are forced to show that such use is not really identical with suprahistorical or supratemporal, and that we are not surreptitiously introducing metaphysical categories into the discussion. Thus, there does not seem to be a middle position between the suprahistorical or supratemporal, on the one hand, and the historical or temporal, on the other. If we start with the presupposition that God must be shown as present at all costs, then the only logical way of escaping the empiricist's critique is the affirmation that God is metaphysical. But the position is not safe from the empiricist's critique either, for how does one distinguish which metaphysical statements are real and which are myths? One can have recourse to fideism and subjectivism, but the question remains: How does one show that fideism is not myth? How does one test the reliability and truth of suprahistorical or metaphysical statements? Ultimately, one has to ground such statements on the empirical. And in our particular case, i.e., the presence of God, we have to ground presence on the empirical. It would seem, however, that when we try to do so, the attempt likewise becomes fruitless. Many intelligent people are therefore led to conclude that God is unreal because his presence cannot be shown.

Part of the current difficulty in trying to show the presence of God proceeds from asking the wrong question. We should redirect the whole effort from trying to show the reality of God by his presence to showing his reality by his absence. This means abandoning the pattern of thinking which situates being in the present. The past is no longer being, the future is not yet. The present is thus made the region of being and also of presence. Now, if the present is the place of the real, then, logically, we would demand that the most real of beings be in the present. Accordingly, efforts to show the reality of God have been to show his presence in the present. It is this framework which has guided not only traditional theists but also the linguistic analysts in the way they ask questions about God. The linguistic analysts are really Aristotelians at heart and mind, for they demand that the verification of the truth and falsity of a statement be the existence of an extramental correlate in the present. Even for them, the present is being. They haven't learned to think and speak evolutionarily.

Jürgen Moltmann confirms our opinion when he observes that traditional knowledge of God was based on the category of the Greek *logos*—hence, a reality which is always there, now and always.[6] Moltmann contrasts this hellenic view with the scriptural view in which God is a God with "future as his essential nature" as made known in Exodus and in Israelite prophecy.[7] Consequently, God is a God we cannot "have" but can only await in active hope.[8] Johann-Baptist Metz also points out that God is a "God before us." [9] We can also add that another image in the Scriptures of God's absence is that of the Lord of the vineyard who is away on a journey but promises to come back. Yahweh is therefore a *Deus Absconditus* (a hidden God), a God Who Cometh.

In accordance with the scriptural view of God, then, our task as theists is to show the reality of God by his absence, not by his presence. Moltmann seems to confirm this new direction when he says:

But now the more recent theology of the Old Testament has indeed shown that the words and statements about the "revealing God" in the Old Testament are combined throughout with statements about the "promise of God." God reveals himself in the form of promise and in the history that is marked by promise. This confronts systematic theology with the question whether the understanding of divine revelation by which it is governed must not be dominated by the nature and trend of the promise.[10]

In the New Testament, adds Moltmann, God is known and described as the "God of promise" (Heb 10:23; 11:11) and God of hope (Rom 15:13).[11]

By redirecting our thinking about God to his absence rather than to his presence, we not only portray the true God of the Scriptures but make him more credible. This may be a surprising thing to say, but paradoxically enough it is true. For if we try to claim that God is present but cannot give evidence of his presence, then God becomes incredible. However, if we, as we should, claim that God is absent and we are able to show good reasons why he is absent, then God becomes credible. We can just as well explain the reality of someone by giving reasons why he is absent than by the evidence of his presence.

In order to give credibility for God's absence, we must answer some nagging questions which are perfectly justified. For example, a question that comes not only from unbelievers but also from believers is why, if the Christian God wanted to win all to his service, does he not make the task easier for himself and his followers by showing some clear evidence of his presence, so that there could be no doubt about it even for sincere men, rather than remaining hidden and forever being a mystery. Is the Christian God a shy God? Does he have a passion for hiddenness? Why does he not come in person and present himself for all to see so that the issue that divides theists and atheists would be solved?

In the previous chapters of this book we have shown that God is a Creator-Ground, a Ground of Growth, and a Ground-Omega. But when all is said and done, the most evident aspect of God is his inevidence. We have no experience of this Creator-Ground, or Ground of human temporality or Ground-Omega. There is no empirical evidence of him in the present. Does it follow that the God we have presented is unreal? Yes, if his reality depended upon the evidence of his presence. What we should do then is to show why God is absent.

The Christian God would be more real and also more human if it were shown that he is absent, not because he wants to, but because of the nature of the situation. The Christian God does not want to be absent for absence' sake, for as the Scriptures attest, the desire and the delight of Yahweh is to be with the children of men, to walk with them. It is just that he cannot help it, given the present situation. It is this situation that we must show. We must give a credible explanation also for faith, and show that faith is not based on the fancy of God as to what the present situation would be, but rather that the present situation determines that faith be characteristic of it.

Let us attempt now to show the reason for God's absence. First, let us put ourselves into the evolutionary pattern of thinking by briefly recalling the ontological dimensions of reality-as-process as shown in the diagram below:

past	present	future
non-being	becoming	being

Corresponding to the ontological dimensions are the revelatory dimensions illustrated thus:

past	present	future
total absence	half-present half-absent	presence
darkness night	twilight night and day	light day

Corresponding to the revelatory dimensions are the cognitive levels or dimensions of reason, shown thus:

past	present	future
"unbelieving" reason	believing reason	seeing reason
science	faith or belief	vision

In the diagrams above, we are situated in the present. This present includes the simple historical future, so that the term "present" is contrasted with the eschatological future. Now, according to the ontological dimensions of process, God, who by presupposition is the most really real, would be located in the absolute future, for that is the region of the fullness of reality. God therefore could not be located in the present, for it is not the region of the fullness of being. By way of contrast, in a static atemporal pattern of thinking, in which the context does not affect essentially the nature of being, it is indifferent to a given being into which ontological dimensions of reality-in-process it is placed. However, if evolution is valid, then a being is determined, not only ontologically, but epistemologically, by the evolutionary stage it is in. Thus, a seed is a seed precisely because it is located at the first stage of the process. It would be absurd to say that the seed could be found in any stage of the process. In fact, the seed is identical with the first stage and is defined as the first stage of this particular process. What is true of individual processes is true of the macrocosmic process of evolution. Thus, man is man precisely because he emerged at a particular stage of the evolutionary process. And matter is matter precisely because it is situated at the first stage of the process. Man has his own dimension, the historical dimension or level of noogenesis, which distinguishes him from the infrahuman levels. Matter, a plant or an animal cannot enter the historical dimension because it does not have self-consciousness and freedom. Or to put it in another way, to be in the historical dimension is to be human. Thus, the ontological dimension determines what a being is ontologically and defines it.

Having shown that the ontological dimension defines the being at that level, let us now study the dimension of the present. The present stage of any given process, that is, the stage of becoming, has the essential characteristics of being half-developed, half-revealing, half-concealing, in short, imperfect and absent from the fullness of being in the future. The significance of these characteristics for our problem is that they determine how a given reality is to appear in it. Let us illustrate what we mean by the use of the example of the seed. In its process of growth, the seed has the following stages:

stage of becoming or the present	stage of being or the future
seed (alpha)	fruit (omega)

In the diagram, in order for the fruit to appear at alpha, it cannot appear in its omega presentation, that is, as fruit. It has to take on the appearance of the seed, which means that the fruit has to be concealed or hidden, so to speak. The structure of alpha prescribes the way omega is to appear at alpha. For omega to appear as omega at alpha is tantamount to putting an end to alpha, since for alpha to become omega is precisely for it to have reached the fullness of maturity or the end of the process. But if omega is serious and intent about the evolution of alpha, then for it to appear at alpha without destroying the structure of alpha, it must appear in the trappings of alpha, as it were. In other words, the result of the "incarnation" of omega in alpha is a descent or *kenosis,* a concealment and an absence from the future, such that the very proof of the presence of omega in alpha is precisely its absence. To demand that for omega to really exist, it present itself as omega at alpha is to deny the very nature of the process as evolutionary. This demand could come only from a static-minded person. In evolution, the very structure of alpha demands the absence of omega in its formal and full presentation at alpha. Thus, in the context of process, we see why omega must paradoxically reveal its presence by its absence, which is the same as to say that omega is present at alpha symbolically. Now, a symbol is a proof of the existence of an absent object. The symbol, in the context of process, points to omega; it half-reveals, half-conceals. At alpha, the only kind of proof for omega is precisely the character of alpha itself as symbolic.

With the above analysis, we are now in a position to understand God's absence in the present. God's revelation of himself must be seen as a process whose fullness is in the absolute future and whose beginning is none other than creation. If this is true, then in the present God could not appear in his total glory and majesty but would have to hide himself in much the same way that the fruit hides itself in the seed. Just as the fruit is in a totally different context or dimension from that of the seed, so God is in a different time dimension. What follows from this is that God cannot totally identify himself with the present order without destroying it. God who is the Fullness of Being could not be in a region of lack and absence of being. God who is the Fullness of Time could not be in the region of lack of time. God who is the Fully Real cannot be in the present which is the region of the partly real. God who is the "I am" cannot be in the present which is the stage of "may be." The present is the region of the contingent, the possible, the subjunctive, the contradictory. It does not have full actuality; it could fail to reach its omega or future. God is none of these. God who is the Fullness of Actuality could not be in a region of becoming. God who is the Fullness of Light could not be in the region of night and day without putting an end to the darkness. God who is the Fullness of Truth could not be in the region of partial truth. God who is Presence could not be in the region of half-presence, half-absence.

God cannot appear in the present order in his total glory and majesty, for this would mean the total destruction of the present. It would be the end of the world, the final judgment, the parousia. It would be like the seed becoming a fruit, which means the destruction of the structure of the seed and the emergence of a new one, the fruit. But as long as the seed exists as a seed, then the fruit cannot incarnate itself at that dimension precisely as fruit. Similarly, for God to come precisely as Omega in our present order would mean the removal of contradiction in the present, the maturation of time, and the removal of all concealment, hiddenness and all darkness. It would mean the final transfiguration and transformation of the present order and the ushering in of a New Age, a New Order, a New Heaven and a New Earth. But as long as God wants the world to evolve, as long as the world is in need of development, then God cannot come in his total glory and majesty.

Does it mean that God cannot be present in some way in our present order? God can come into the present but in a concealed way. This is the only way he can come into the present without destroying the character of the present as evolving. He cannot come, as we already mentioned, in his character and function as Judge, as Omega, if he allows both "cockle and wheat to grow." God has to assume the character of the present by putting aside the glory of his divinity. Because the revelatory dimension of the present is the region of night and day, all things in the present order partake of this character—they are half-light, half-intelligible, half-revealing. In other words, the present is a symbol of the eschatological future. God's presence, then, in the present order is in the form of symbols. As the revelation of God evolves through time, the symbols become more and more revealing of him, much as the development of the seed manifests more and more of its final form. The Scriptures in fact attest to the presence of God in history in terms of symbols. First, creation itself is a symbol of God, a vestige of God. Then man himself as an image of God becomes a clearer symbol of God. But God did not stop at man as a revelation of himself. He chose a still fuller revelation of himself by choosing a people in which he manifested himself through his saving acts. From this people, he chose types of himself—Abraham, Moses, David—and finally he sent the perfect symbol of himself, his only Son.

Corresponding to the absence of God-Omega in the present is the character of faith as an experience of absence. In this experience of absence, the reality of God is implied, but not the presence of God, since man is a wayfarer, dwelling in tents, away from the Lord. He is on a journey, an exodus toward God who dwells in inaccessible light (1 Tim 6:16), with the light of faith as his guide amid the darkness. It is the condition of the journey or exodus, or, as we expressed in the first chapter of this study, the unfinished character of the present—that is the foundation of belief, and not the whim of God. Belief is necessary because it is the only way we can recognize the Future where Truth is found and be open to it. It has often been said and taught that in belief we attain God's presence. This is true in the sense that belief relates us to the Absolute Future, makes us recognize it, but not in the sense that in belief we attain a religious experience of God. No, faith is darkness in relation to the Absolute Future which is the region of day. The substance of faith, precisely, is the eschatological hope that eventually the rhythm of darkness and light will give way to an eternal day, when God will be his people's light (Is 30:26; 60:19-22; Hos 6:3; Zech 14:7;

cf. Eccl 12:2; Is 2:1; Rev 21:23; 22:5).[12] For the Christian, Christ's coming announces the dawn of a New Age, which will never be followed by a night (Rev 21:23; 22:5).[13]

Faith is not all darkness, but darkness only in relation to the eschaton. In relation to unborn or unbelieving reason, faith is a light. As St. John says, those who do not believe remain in darkness (Jn 3:19-21), while those who believe are children of light (Jn 1:12-13; 12:36). We may illustrate the paradoxical nature of faith as being both light and darkness or presence and absence thus:

unbelieving reason   →   faith or believing reason
(darkness or absence)   (light or presence)

faith   →   vision
(darkness or absence)   (light or presence)

In the diagram, faith in relation to unborn reason is a light; it is a presence in the sense of a recognition of the reality of God. But faith in relation to vision, which is light or presence, is darkness or absence. This paradoxical nature of faith cannot be recognized in the static pattern of thought which is based on the logic of the identity of concepts. Thus, faith cannot be both light and darkness, presence and absence. Historically, what was emphasized was the triumphalistic aspect of faith, rather than its eschatological or futuristic dimension. Faith was seen exclusively as an experience of the presence of God, with the result that not only the false hopes of unbelievers were aroused and a crisis of faith in believers induced but also a wrong direction on the question of God of looking for a datum of God's presence was initiated in theology. As Moltmann brings out, God is the not-yet-datum-for-us; God is he-who-is-to-come. Therefore, the search for a datum, be it metaphysical, existential or intuitive, cannot yield an experience of God.

The man of faith lives in a paradoxical situation. He is unable to give a datum for his belief in God—hence, belief seems irrational to reason. But for the man of faith, the light of faith is a surer light than that of reason to guide man on his journey toward the Absolute Future. Having said this, we must also say that the life of faith in relation to the life of vision is one of darkness, for we do not yet see the consummation of which faith gives the certainty.[14] Again, in relation to reason, faith gives freedom, security, and deliverance from despair (Gal 4:1-5:13; Rom 6:12-19; Eph 2:1-5; Col 3:5-10; 1 Thes 4:3-9, etc.), but in relation to the eschaton, faith is the experience of fear, of doubt and of absence, for, precisely, the Christian walks by faith, not by vision (2 Cor 5:7). Because in relation to vision, faith is absence, faith requires constant affirmation. It needs to be nurtured, for it is in process of growth toward final qualitative transformation into the life of vision and glory.

The Exodus account pictures very well the paradoxical experience of the life of faith. The Israelites at once felt free and yet unfree: free from the slavery of Egypt, but not yet free from the dangers of the desert. They were secure and yet not secure, alive and yet not quite alive, happy and yet still sorrowing, certain and yet also uncertain and doubtful of the outcome of the journey. Compared to the darkness of Egypt, a pillar of light was given them, but before them on the way to the land of truth and light was darkness. The food given them in the desert was "manna" which was quite unpalatable and tasteless, compared to the fleshpots of Egypt. As a consequence, many succumbed to the temptation of going back to Egypt and, in the attempt, died on the way or reverted back to slavery. So, too, the life of faith is a life of emptiness and darkness in the desert where one's truth and certainty as food for the journey are not a verifiable and present truth but a promise, just as the manna was a promise of the land flowing with milk and honey. To reason, the truth of faith is unpalatable, for it does not give a "taste" of God. Reason could fall into the temptation of going back to the security of its concepts, proclaiming that God-talk is meaningless. This brings us to the problem of the validity of God-language.

In the introduction to this study, we attempted to establish the empirical foundation for religious language. We stated there that the eschatological dimension is the foundation for religious talk. God-talk, not only because it is part of religious talk, but also because God (which is the object of God-talk) is he-who-comes, is also founded on the eschatological dimension of reality. As Moltmann points out, God-language must be set in the category of expectation, since this is appropriate for a God of promise.[15] Our problem here, therefore, is not to establish the ontological foundation for God-talk but to consider the position and claim of linguistic analysis in relation to the question of the validity of God-talk.

One of the most formidable allies of the death-of-God movement is the group of linguistic analysts who claim that God-talk is cognitively meaningless. There are other linguistic analysts, however, who are moving away from the extreme and strict notion of the verification principle. I believe that the movement is welcome. I even see in it the possibility that in the future, linguistic analysis will be of great service to the clarification of religious language. At the present time, then, the task is to broaden the scope and meaning of linguistic analysis so that it can be of service to religious language and, in our particular case, to God-language.

A philosopher notes three areas in which linguistic philosophy could broaden itself: [16] (1) broaden the verifiability principle so as to make other experiences besides sense experience possible, (2) abandon the viewpoint that would reduce all meaning of things to present or actual fact, and

(3) pay more attention to conceptual frameworks through which we seek to apprehend the world.

I would concur with the above suggestions, but I would reduce the three points to one: the development of a philosophy of language in the context of an evolving universe. My basic dissatisfaction with linguistic analysis is its static nature. It is valid for a static universe in which present facts alone count and the future is considered of no linguistic value or is reduced to present statements and in which reason is considered statically, that is, as adequate and sufficient for attaining all the meaning there is, when, as a matter of fact, reason is evolving. My second basic dissatisfaction with linguistic analysis is that, like Aristotelian logic, of which it is heir, it is unable to deal with paradoxes. It considers as a contradiction the statement that a Christian is at once a sinner and a just man (*simul justus et peccator*). It cannot deal with the paradoxical nature of presently evolving realities but must freeze them, as it were, in order to make sense out of them.

Religious language is of a paradoxical nature, as when it is said that Christ is both God and man, that the Christian is at once free and unfree, already born and yet unborn, etc. Religious language is also historical and evolutionary: it depicts the people of God as on a journey to the holy land, the Church as a mystical body evolving toward the fullness of Christ, the liturgy as consisting of cycles of growth, the Christian life as an exodus, grace as growth in the fullness of Christ, dogma as evolving, etc.

It is necessary, then, to develop a philosophy of language that would take account of the nature of religious language rather than taking scientific language as a model and *a priori* presupposing that religious language is cognitively meaningless, then trying to explain its meaning in terms of non-cognitive, non-factual and emotive uses.

I would like to begin the examination of the validity of the linguistic method for determining the validity of God-talk by a clarification of what is meant by the terms "empirical," "truth," "verifiability" and "reason." If the universe is evolving, then these terms must be seen in this context. Most linguistic analysts take these terms for granted when any true scientific procedure would require their clarification as a necessary step to their proper use in language.

What is meant by the truly empirical? Can we really establish an empirical fact? What is a fact? I would start by proposing a definition of an empirical fact as that whose existence cannot be contested. Now, in terms of this definition, what example can we give for an empirical fact? The tree out there which I sense and experience? But that tree out there is open toward the future; hence, its existence is uncertain, contested by future life or death. But perhaps it is asserted that apart from the future and death, the tree exists. The notion of an empirical fact, however, as pointing to the present alone, is an abstraction, existing only in the mind or to common sense, for all things in time cannot be thought of apart from their futures. Remove the future and the present has no existence of its own that may be called autonomous and incontestable. A tree without a future is a dead tree. It is no longer a tree. Reflection shows that the basis for presently existing things is really their future.[17] What is it then to be empirical? To answer this question properly, it must be set in the context of the real world which is evolving. Now, since in evolution the direction is toward greater being in the future, it follows that the future is more empirical than the present. It might be objected that since the future does not yet exist, how can it be empirical? The present does exist; hence it is empirical. But the existence of the present is not due to the present but to there being a future. It could be that the future is never reached, in which case the present ceases to be and hence leaves no basis for talk. True empiricism then is based on a realized future, that is, on the achievement of maturity or the fullness of growth, for a realized future does not need to have a future in the line of this particular present growth. The present, then, as becoming or as evolving, is not fully empirical. Because it is an abstraction, it is false to compare the present with the future, for they are not two entities, the present having existence and hence empirical, while the future, having no existence, is not empirical. That the present does not have autonomous existence is clear by what we have said, namely that if the future is taken away from it, it ceases to be. The present, then, is not truly and fully empirical; it is empirical only thanks to the future and because of its participation in the future. If this is true, it is false to reduce the future to the present, making the present the model of the empirical and of what is real.

The implication of our analysis for God-talk is that it would be false to demand that God be found in the present, precisely because the present is not the region of the fully empirical. Hence, to use the present and its language structure as a basis for verifying whether God is real or not is doomed to fail, for God, who by presupposition is the most fully empirical, cannot be found in the region that is partially empirical.

Just as the fullness of empiricism is the stage of maturation in the future, since that is the region of the fullness of being, so also the region of the fullness of truth is the future, since truth is convertible with being. Linguistic analysis, on the other hand, locates truth in the present. For it, that is true which exists extramentally here and now. In this sense, everything that emerges from non-existence is true, but this statement is a tautology and does not say anything new. It starts from a dualism between being and non-being, asserting that the region of being is true. What is at fault here is a static view of the real, such that there is no distinction made between authentic and inauthentic being in which the former is true and the latter false. In linguistic analysis, that is true which exists, and that false which does not. But this usage is tautological. For truth and falsity to be meaningful, they both must have extramental references. To speak of a non-existent being as meaningless or false is to be tautological. In evolution, on the other hand, true and false both have extramental references. That is true which has attained the fullness of its growth. Truth is equated with the successful completion and maturation of a process. Untruth is in incompletion or death. For example, a seed that is not planted is untrue because, left alone, it will soon shrivel up and die. It is tautological to say the seed is true simply because it exists. Truth, for the seed, is reaching its maturation. In line with evolutionary thinking, a developing reality is half-true because it has not yet reached its fullness or maturation. The present, then, which is a stage of becoming, is the region of half-truth.

If our previous analysis is true, then in relation to God-talk it would be invalid and fruitless to apply the method of linguistic analysis to verify God's presence in the present, for God who is the Fullness of Truth could not be found in the region of half-truth. God could be found and empirically verified only in the Absolute Future, for that is the region of the fullness of truth.

Let us next examine the notion of verifiability. We can verify things that are present to us, so that presence, obviously, is the basis for verifiability. But when is a thing present? This seems a silly question, but only to common sense, which, contrary to the popular view, is quite unphilosophical. Thus, to common sense, a seed in front of me is present. But is it really present in and for itself? Or, to phrase the question in a more general way, is the developing or evolving present really present in, by and for itself? Our analysis previously has shown that the present has existence only because it has a future, that if the future were sheared off, the present would cease to be present; it would be handed over to death or non-existence. The present, in the context of evolution, being unfinished, half-developed, is not fully present to itself. The future is still unrevealed. What follows from this is that there are realities unseen or unrevealed in the present. If this is true, then we are not able to verify absolutely whether a given reality which does not appear in the present really exists or not. All we can say is that the given reality does not appear in the present. We cannot say absolutely that it does not exist. For proper and adequate verification, we must situate ourselves in a place where all things are present. Only then can we say whether what we are verifying is real or unreal.

The implication of our analysis of verifiability for God-talk is that since the present is the region of half-presence, half-absence, of light and darkness, day and night, then God who is Presence and Light cannot be found in the present. God is absent from the present, not because he does not exist but because the present is absence in relation to the Absolute Future which is the region of presence. To verify Presence, we must go to the region of presence. The present, paradoxically enough, is not the region of presence.

Not only is the present incapable of verifying the reality of God, but also the tool for verification, namely, unevolved reason, is incapable of the job. Only reason reborn to faith can attain the reality of God. Thus, we see the logic and validity of the claims of a reason reborn to faith that one must first believe in order to verify the reality of God.

Now to a static mind, there is a difficulty in understanding the proper role of faith. It thinks that faith is a super-addition to reason. It thinks that to call upon faith as an aid to reason is really an abandonment of reason, and hence unreasonable.

But our point is that reason is an evolving reality, hence unfinished, and that, therefore, there is a future to reason. It is this future dimension of reason which we call faith. Therefore, faith is none other than reason, but it is reason reborn to a new dimension. Thus, we are not bringing in an extrinsic criterion; faith is intrinsic to reason, in fact, its "within" or innermost depths. It is static philosophy which influenced both traditional theology and linguistic analysis that is responsible for the dualism between reason and faith, because it considers reason as given fully finished, fully adequate for its role. True, it must be considered fully finished and fully adequate in a static universe; otherwise the creator would be considered unwise and improvident for creating a deficient tool. But in an evolving universe, it is possible to have an unfinished tool; in fact, it is demanded by the context without implying that the maker is unwise, since he allows for the evolution of things in time. Now, since linguistic analysts consider reason sufficient and adequate, faith becomes illogical or at least extrinsic to reason. What we are proposing as a more adequate tool for the verification of the reality of God is believing reason, since it reaches the eschatological future where the reality of God can be discovered. We are therefore appealing from reason unborn to reason-born-to-the-dimension-of-faith to judge adequately the validity of God-talk.

Let us say a few words here on the nature of language in the developing present. The language of the present is that of symbols. Symbols point to the future for their reality; hence they are relative, provisional and always couched in the subjunctive mood because there is the dimension of futurity and possibility in them. Only in the future where being is firmly possessed can there be a true assertion, an assertion in the indicative mood.[18] Because the future has the indicative statement, it is in a position to judge the truth of the present, and not the other way around, as the linguistic analysts seem to have presupposed. But this linguistic view is an unreflected view, supported only by common sense. Common sense would consider the present the place of the real while the future is reduced to the present. Ordinary language based on the common-sense view would speak of the future coming: the coming hour, day, week, year, event, etc. The truth, however, is that the present tends toward the future.

Ordinary language and scientific language by their very nature abstract from ultimate questions. Religious language, on the other hand, deals with ultimate and eschatological questions. For the eschatological dimension, we cannot use scientific or ordinary models of language. In the present, as linguistic analysts have seen, God-talk is neither verifiable nor falsifiable. But it is false to conclude that therefore God-talk is meaningless in itself.

6

GOD AND
HUMAN FREEDOM

S artre has expressed the objection of many to the Christian God when he said that God is a threat to man's freedom, for if man is creative of himself, the independent and sovereign creator of his own destiny, then God is not his creator. In other words, if man is absolute freedom as Sartre would define man, then God could not be his lawgiver, for that would restrict human freedom. This implies that God could not be the creator of a human nature in which he imprints a natural law that man must obey. In short, there cannot be true freedom if man's existence is simply the realization of some pre-conceived plan or decree external to man.

Marxism, too, sees the Christian God as a threat to man's freedom. Adam Schaff in "Modern Marxism and the Individual." [1] speaks of "old Jehovah" as cruel and the Christian miserable. Thus he says:

> This miserable worm, with such means of knowledge at his command as the Ten Commandments, racks his brains as to what to do in life's conflicting situations

and lives in a state of discord and fear, only to earn condemnation at the end. And yet this miserable and helpless creature, worthy of both pity and contempt, is in the light of religion the sovereign individual, God's highest creation! Atheistic and religious Existentialism alike repeat the tale of the cruelty and maliciousness of the old Jehovah. They create their individual as supposedly sovereign in order to make him lonely. They condemn to helplessness and despair the wretched puppets who are the sport of malicious fate while wearing the hollow crown of "sovereignty."

Given this view of God as malicious and cruel and one who makes puppets of men, the Marxists try to do away with God dialectically by showing that God does not create man but that man creates God in his own image.[2]

Another thinker who proclaims the death of God because he destroys human freedom is Nietzsche. He asks: "What could one create if gods existed? . . . The God who saw everything, even man—this God had to die." [3] Thus, according to Nietzsche, man's creativity and capacity for dynamic growth are destroyed by the fixed gaze of this eternal look; it freezes the free becoming of the future into a determined dead fate.

And Sigmund Freud adds "some psychological foundation to the criticisms of [his] great predecessors" that God destroyed human creativity and growth by asserting that religion is "the universal obsessional neurosis of humanity; like the obsessional neurosis of children, it arose out of the Oedipus complex, out of the relation to the father. If this view is right, it is to be supposed that a turning away from religion is bound to occur with the fatal inevitability of a process of growth, and that we find ourselves at this very juncture in the middle of that phase of development." [4]

We can say as a general answer to the above criticisms that what they are actually objecting to is the God of classical theism, the God who is other-worldly, timeless, the God who makes paper plates. But a denial of that God is not necessarily a denial of God.

As a general critique of the existentialism of Nietzsche and Sartre and the psychological analysis of Freud, we might observe that their anthropology is too narrow because it is static and non-evolutionary. To get a proper and adequate understanding of human freedom, one has to see man in the total context of evolution, for freedom did not start with man; it had its evolutionary roots at the infrahuman level. Man is not a Cartesian thinking substance. So against Sartre, we say that man is not merely a self-constituting free (indeterminate) consciousness, the ultimate and sufficient source of creativity. Man also derives his meaning from his pre-historical past, an important source for any adequate and valid anthropology, but which the existentialists do not consider. The Marxists consider man's evolutionary past, but because they are encumbered by the Aristotelian concept of a self-sufficient nature of which they are unconscious heirs, they fail to analyze properly the causality involved in the evolutionary process and as a result arrive at an adequate anthropology.

But the root cause of the opinion that God is a threat to human creativity is due not to a defect in logic but to the false assumptions derived from a static frame of reference that pictures God as a metaphysical and Transcendent Other, and this world as an autonomous natural order. It is static thinking that portrays God as a creator of fixed, static and immutable essences and which is the root cause of modern man's irreligious attitude. Modern non-religious man is rebelling against a false notion of God, but his alternative position, unfortunately enough, still derives from a dualism, only that now he chooses man over God. Mircea Eliade de-

scribes very well the position of modern non-religious man
as follows:

> Modern non-religious man assumes a new existential
> situation; he regards himself solely as the subject and
> agent of history, and he refuses all appeal to transcen-
> dence. In other words, he accepts no model for humanity
> outside the human condition as it can be seen in the
> various historical situations. *Man makes himself*, and
> he only makes himself completely as he desacralizes him-
> self and the world. The sacred is the prime obstacle to
> his freedom. He will become himself only when he is
> totally demysticized. He will not be truly free until he
> has killed the last god.[5]

Here we have the same old problem of transcendence versus
immanence, metaphysical versus the existential-historical—
a problem which cannot be resolved within the hellenic frame
of reference, without sacrificing one to the other. A Christian
within such a static frame of reference might perhaps argue
against the existentialist (who is also in this frame) that the
Christian God is not a watchmaker or maker of paper plates,
that God does not destroy human creativity. But all such
assertions are ineffective in stemming the tide of modern
atheism. What is needed is to get out of this frame of reference. Both traditionalists (metaphysicians) and existentialists
have to learn to think evolutionarily. We have to situate the
problem of God and human creativity within an evolutionary
context.

Let us therefore consider the problem of God and human
freedom within the evolutionary framework. We will consider
first the problem of human creativity, then the relation of
human freedom to God's causality, God's foreknowledge,
and lastly, God's law.

With regard to human creativity, what we need to derive is a new anthropology. We have to reexamine our traditional view of man as his human nature. The difficulty with the view that man already has a human nature is that man cannot be really creative, since all that man could effect in himself would be merely an accidental change in his being. If man is to be truly creative of himself, he must be able to touch his most profound depths; he must be radically open toward the future.

From the Christian point of view, the attempt to show that man does create himself is not an easy one. For if we allow man to create his own destiny, his own essence, then we would seem to be endangering God's creativity with respect to man. God's creative role would seem to be superfluous. The problem for Christians is to reconcile God's creativity and man's creativity in the creation of man. If we cannot achieve this, then the Christian God will appear tyrannical and therefore unlovable.

Let us begin the delineation of the limits of human creativity by first determining certain common and universal elements in man which man did not create. Thus, the emergence of man, a process which might be called anthropogenesis or hominization, is something that man did not create. As a result of the biological process of hominization or anthropogenesis, man is endowed with a "hominized" body and a hominized consciousness. In other words, his body is not an animal but a human body, and his consciousness is not animal consciousness but human consciousness. Man is therefore an ex-animal. It is possible that in the future, man's creativity may touch this level of hominization, resulting in more intelligent, taller, individuals with pre-determined temperaments, etc. However, it is not on the level of hominization that man's creativity is most properly exercised but on the level of what we might call humanization. Here, it is not a question of the emergence of man from the animal, but the emergence of a humanized individual from the hominized form.

Let us try to specify more precisely the sphere of humanization. Thus, over and above the biological process of hominization is the process of personalization in which man is no longer a passive product of evolution. Man is now evolution conscious of itself. He is now able to create and to direct evolution itself. This sphere of creativity is the sphere of history and culture. This is what man creates. Teilhard de Chardin calls this level the noosphere, and the process of creativity, that of noogenesis. On this level, man does not have a form yet. Man is not born, at this level, human. He must humanize himself. In contrast, at the lower level of hominization, man is born in hominized form. He does not have to create this form.

The difference between the two levels is that in the hominization process, the evolution is from the pre-historical (animal) to the historical (man as "rational animal"). In the process of humanization, on the other hand, the evolution takes place within the context of the historical, from an uncivilized, impersonal, inhuman historical situation, for example, to a civilized, interpersonal and more human one. This distinction might help us resolve the issue as to whether essence precedes existence or existence precedes essence.

In the traditional view of man, essence precedes existence. In other words, man is endowed with a human nature which then determines the way man is going to act. Man's essence is a given. The level of history becomes purely accidental and secondary. In the historicist and existential view of man, "existence comes before essence." [6] There is no *a priori* human nature.[7] Sartre denies the possibility of finding "in each and every man a universal essence that can be called a human nature." [8] He does not deny that there is a human universality of condition, that is, "all the limitations which *a priori* define man's fundamental situation in the universe," namely, "the necessities of being in the world, of having to labor and to die there." [9] These situations are not in man, however, as his essence, for to say this is to destroy the radical possibility of man constituting himself. Essence cannot precede existence. Man is unique among realities of the world, for he first exists and make free decisions before he can be defined.[10]

The issue just described is unresolvable as long as we stay within a static frame of reference. We cannot say that both sides are correct. We must accept one and deny the other. The current trend has been to accept the existential-historical view with the result that in theology the existential is preferred to the metaphysical, and in morality, the situational to the objective.

Again we run into the basic problem of transcendence vs. immanence. We have to get out of the static framework which forces us to distinguish the metaphysical and the historical spatially or vertically. We have to get into the evolutionary framework where they can be seen horizontally or temporally, to allow for relativity in the concepts. Thus, the notion of "essence" as used by the metaphysical view of man must be historicized, must be seen relatively. It is not timeless. To see this, let us use an illustration we used before:

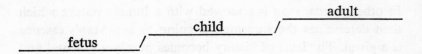

In the illustration, the emergence or development of the child is a permanent achievement in relation to the fetus. The child is essentialy a distinct form compared to the more quantitative form of growth of the fetus. But in relation to the adult, the form of the child is relative. It is not an "essence" in the metaphysical sense; it is evolutionary, or historical, if you will. Similarly, by comparing man with an animal, we speak of him as a "rational animal." The difference is not merely one of condition or situation, but an essential difference. If it were merely a difference in condition, then to put an animal in the same condition as man should make him a man, which is patently false. The so-called conditions of man are intrinsic to man; they are non-transferable, which is the same as to say that they are "essential" to man. In relation to the animal then, we can speak of a human nature that is common to every man, but we must be careful to make the qualification that this is a relative "essence." Man is still in process, at the level of noogenesis, so he has a future. In relation to that future, man does not yet have his essence or nature. Man is much more than a "rational animal." We are not saying that man has two natures; we are saying that the "rational animal" will be transcended, just as the child form is transcended by the adult form. In the metaphysical view, any future form is always accidental, the finished form being the hominized form we get from comparing man to the animal. But from the point of view of the higher stage of noogenesis, the hominized form, "rational animal," is but a provisional form. The final form is still to be achieved and constituted. This is man's true definition and not the so-called metaphysical definition of man as a "rational animal" which upon reflection is quite relative and really biological. The basis of the final definition is in terms of personality, love, regard for others. It is through love that the true and intrinsic nature of man is constituted. In terms of this norm, when we are born we are not yet men. We constitute ourselves men in the moral and human sense of the term. This nature is not accidental to man; if he does not attain it, then he is not truly a man even if biologically he is one. The metaphysical statement that man who changes remains always a man is true biologically, but not at the historical-human level. For example, a man even after committing the most terrible and atrocious of crimes against humanity remains a man biologically; he is still a "rational animal"—i.e., essentially distinct from an animal—but within the context of society, he does not belong.

With the evolutionary view and distinction, we are able to accept the biological definition of man as a "rational animal." Without the distinction, the existentialists are forced to deny that essence precedes existence. But in a sense it is true that essence precedes existence in that man is indeed distinct essentially from an animal. In another sense, it is also true to say that existence precedes essence, and the metaphysical view is consequently wrong in denying it, for essence in this case is defined within the world of interpersonal relationships, within the world of history and human society, within the world of reason itself which Teilhard would call the noosphere. Within this world, we do not compare man with an animal; rather, we compare him with what he ought to be in order to be truly human. In this new dimension, man is not born human; he must humanize himself; he is not born rational; there is still much of the irrational and inhuman in him as history—recent history—abundantly testifies. Man must therefore create his essence, and it is this essence that counts for man, not the fact that he is distinct from the animal.

The Christian then is not necessarily committed to a metaphysical view of man in which God must appear as a threat to human creativity. In fact, the biblical view of man is not metaphysical at all. It is closer to the existential view than to the traditional one. As exegetes assert, "the likeness of man is not to be drawn from something called 'human nature.' " [11] In the New Testament, to know man, "it is not enough to describe him in terms of natural phenomena, biological development or psychological individuality. Man is a person. He must be known in his relations with others and in his particular setting in the history of humanity—that environment which reacts to his behavior and in which he exercises responsible action. . . . The true perspective of the N.T. always shows man in community and in history." [12]

The metaphysical view of man has clouded the most important task for man—the search for and the constitution of freedom. Since we have identified man with the definition "rational animal" and taken this to be the end point of what it is to be man, we have also identified freedom in man with the possession of free choice. We conclude that man is free. Again, this is quite true as long as we are distinguishing man from animals. Yes, man is free because he is endowed with free choice. But in terms of the goal of humanization, the constitution of a person, the conquest of tyrannical passions— fear, hate, prejudice, ignorance—the internal "I" is not free. Free choice is not the end; it is the beginning of freedom. It is not merely to be used for the actualization of certain accidental perfections which serve as ornament for human nature; it is for the constitution of the very substance, the very meaning of man.

The common man usually identifies freedom with free choice. When teenagers, for example, cry for freedom, they usually mean free choice to be able to do anything they want. This notion of freedom is the freedom of our first definition of man as a "rational animal." But the possession of an intellect and will does not *ipso facto* constitute man free, in the second sense of the term. In this second sense, which is usually unknown to the common man, man is not born free. He must work to become free internally. To use an example, Hitler, insofar as he has free choice, is free, but insofar as he has sunk to the level of the animal by becoming irrational and inhuman, he is not free. Not every free choice results in freedom. One who sinks to the level of the animal, who surrenders himself to every passing whim and fancy, passion and vice, is not free. We must work to become free. The Scriptures also consider man as still unfree; he is still in the state of internal slavery to sin and to the tyranny of the passions. Man is solemnly warned that his ultimate success and destiny is in fashioning and constituting the new man (Rom 8:29; 2 Cor 3:18), in creating a new humanity (1 Cor 15:20-23; Col 1:18; Eph 4:15).

Basically, it is this hellenic formulation of man that Sartre, Marx, Feuerbach and Freud were against, not the true biblical view. But even with the biblical view that man must create himself, these critics take issue in the sense that they maintain that man alone makes himself. As Eliade has observed, the modern non-religious man wants complete autonomy and independence in creating and constituting himself, and that therefore God is a threat to this enterprise. God is a threat in three ways: (1) man ceases to be the sole creator of his essence, (2) God's foreknowledge does not really make the future open, and (3) God's laws and commandments preclude human self-determination.

The conclusions of these critics, I believe, are the result of taking a too narrow perspective within which to observe man's creativity. To get an adequate understanding of human creativity, an evolutionary standpoint should be taken. To answer the question whether God is a threat to human freedom, we must first ask the question what it is to be free, what the forces are that we must conquer to attain freedom. It is insufficient to start from a consideration of man alone, using a purely phenomenological or psychoanalytic method, for we are automatically bound by the method with the result that we identify human freedom with psychological maturity from an infantile stage of belief, or with the indeterminism of the self in the constitution and imposition of meaning on the world. Such an analysis becomes anthropomorphic. Human freedom is not man's goal alone, is not man's possession alone, for man is not just his own. Man emerged, thanks to the infrahuman level of evolution. His responsibility is not just to himself but to the whole billions of years of evolution. Human freedom was billions of years in the making. So the infrahuman levels have a say as to what human freedom is.

Human freedom is just the highest point of the evolutionary process. We can justly say that the whole process is the evolution of freedom since the process evolved toward human freedom. Freedom, then, stripped of its human aspects—free choice, social, political, academic and religious freedoms, etc.—is basically freedom from entropy. Entropy is the disintegration and the dissolution of what has been evolved or created. It is the enemy of evolution and creativity. It not only destroys what has been created; it also prevents the possibility of creation and evolution. As evolution and creativity evolve, so does entropy. At the lowest level of the evolutionary process, entropy manifests itself in physical form as the loss or disintegration of physical energy. As material evolution becomes living matter, entropy at this level of life becomes death, which is the cessation of life through the dissolution and decomposition of the living parts. The greater the life, the greater the death. The death of a single cell is not as great as the death of an animal. When we come to man, entropy takes on greater power. It does not mean merely physical death or the death of biological man; it means also the death of personality, or spiritual and moral death—a far greater death, for a life of self-hate is a living death.

Corresponding to the evolution of entropy or the forces of death and enslavement is the evolution of freedom. Thus there is the freedom of the molecule from atomization through the strength derived from union, from more complex arrangement; then there is the freedom of the cell from molecular disintegration by means of nutrition, reproduction, and association with other cells; then there is the greater freedom of more complex living organisms that develop specialized organs to cope with forces of decay and death such as pests, disease, floods, heat, etc. Animals of the more complex type have greater "freedom" compared to plants because they have senses and locomotive powers to sense danger and flee from enemies: floods, heat, drought, etc. Furthermore, by being in groups (herds, colonies) through the gregarious instincts, the animal is better able to preserve its species compared to infraanimal forms of life.

When we come to man, there are evolved greater forces of creativity to cope with the correspondingly greater forces of entropy. For the tyranny of instinct there is the freedom derived from rationality and free choice. With knowledge, man is able to make choices instead of acting from mechanistic and pre-determined instinct or ignorance. With knowledge he can know causes of entropy in himself—e.g., sickness and disease, either physical or mental—and take means to prevent or cure them. With memory and foresight he can better understand his past and his present and better direct himself toward his future goals. For the forces of spiritual entropy or moral decay like fear, hate and prejudice, he has the forces of trust, hope, belief, love and understanding. For great physical and moral strength, man bands together to form societies and thus protect himself by laws and restraints and thus assure his freedom; he pools his knowledge and experience and transmits them to future generations to assure the conquest of ignorance and mistakes.

Freedom then is nothing but the quest for being and life. Now to attain being and life, one has to evolve, for to cease to evolve is the same as to die, which is a loss of freedom, ultimately, for freedom is founded on the possession of being. To evolve is (1) to unite with others and form more complex organization, and (2) to attain full differentiation. What is true of our analysis of the macrocosmic process is also true at the microcosmic or individual level. Thus, in the case of biological man, physical freedom is attained by growing from childhood to adulthood, since freedom of activity is attained by the possession of fully differentiated physical parts. In the case of the fetus, freedom is attained by being freed from the confinement of the womb, achieved through continued union with the womb and growth to fullness. In the case of the seed, freedom is attained by a process of germination. The seed is liberated from its aloneness or existence-toward-death by the ground. The ground gives the seed life and through continued union with the ground, the seed breaks the confinement of the seed coat and is reborn to a new life in the seedling. In the case of the human individual, personality is attained through loving union with others. To build himself up into a person, man must unite and relate himself to others in the community, but at the same time not be swallowed or enslaved by the community which could very well become a power of oppression and enslavement. Before the individual can be properly related to the community and be a force of union and liberation for others, the individual must conquer the forces of moral disintegration in himself; he must be at peace with himself; he must conquer fear, hate suspicion, false judgments, ignorance, prejudice, etc. Without internal freedom man either enslaves others or is enslaved by others.

Freedom then must be seen in the context of life and death. The whole evolutionary process tended toward man in the hope that through human knowledge and free choice man may lead the whole process in the right path that leads to being and life. The question, however, is: Does man have the power to save and liberate the universe from ultimate entropy? Before he can give being and life to the infrahuman levels, man must ask himself whether he can be his own liberator from his own state of slavery and entropy—slavery from physical death and from the forces of moral and personal evil. Is it the case that man will be able to conserve himself, his civilization, his history and the world not only from the ravages of time and death but also from man's own destructive and demonic tendencies? Or will not all this human effort and creativity crumble to dust and be at the mercy of extrinsic forces?

The evolutionary view of Teilhard is that the evolutionary process needs a Ground evolver, as liberator from entropy, as maturer. There is need of a Fullness of Time that is the ultimate source of time and that therefore can liberate the process from the ravages of decay and death. There is need of an Omega or Center of Attraction that will unite all the personal centers of consciousness through the bond of love and thus be a source of liberation from the forces of hate and the demonic in us. Thus, against the proponents of complete autonomy for man, the evolutionary view of Teilhard asserts that freedom is in union, not isolation. The universe is not an autonomous Aristotelian natural order able to achieve its end by its own natural powers. It is a "covenanted" universe where to be free is to be united. Liberation is in union.

The scriptural view is that freedom for man is in entering the covenant. Man is not his own salvation, for, as Paul says (Rom 7), man is impotent. The inward "I" is incapable of real independence; it has no power to do good; it can conceive, it can will the good, but this process remains at the stage of good intentions, of imagination. The source of freedom is the Lord Christ (1 Cor 7:22; 12:13; Gal 3:28). By him all forces of slavery are shaken and vanquished. These forces are forces of internal corruption (2 Pet 2:19; Rom 6:18-23). *The Vocabulary of the Bible* summarizes the role, of Christ as savior:

The "Messiah" comes now to attack the roots of evil, which man neither would nor could eliminate, nor even recognize in himself. He comes to liberate man from himself, to reveal to him that his pretended ("internal") freedom is slavery, to give his life in order to purchase forgiveness, and to rise in order that the way of freedom be opened up. Man resists his own liberation; but he who follows Jesus to the end passes into the world of freedom and into life eternal, even though death may still intervene. . . . For faith and for hope the time of freedom has commenced, and sin and death are already vanquished.[13]

It would seem that if God is the liberator and savior of man, human creativity becomes an empty word. The problem in Christian thought is how to distinguish divine causality from the human and give each one its proper due. In the past we have gone into both extremes: Pelagianism, on the one hand, which overemphasizes human causality and the *ex opere operato* mechanism, on the other, which overemphasizes divine causality to the detriment of human creativity. The difficulty in reconciling the two is that we have no experience of divine causality. In the hellenic framework, the two main theories proposed are those of *pre motio physica* (physical pre-motion) of God, or the divine concursus. We believe that these theories do not properly explain the relation. We prefer to use the analogies furnished by the Scriptures, analogies which are intrinsic to an evolutionary frame of reference. Thus, God's causality or creativity may be compared to the causality of the ground in relation to the seed. The Scriptures compare man to a seed that must die in order to be reborn. Outside the ground, the seed is unable to cause its own growth; it cannot evolve or create itself; it cannot produce its own fruit. Similarly, the Scriptures speak of man outside the covenant (Ground) or outside faith as weak, impotent, fallen (2 Cor 1:12; Rom 6:19), carnal as opposed to the spiritual (1 Cor 15:35-49; Phil 3:21). Man must "die" to his former state of slavery in order to be born a free son of God, just as the seed must die to its isolation, to its separation from the ground in order to attain the new life of the seedling. The creativity of God is on a totally different plane from that of man, as different as the causality of the ground in relation to that of the seed. God is not like a super-seed that helps an ordinary seed to evolve and attain liberation from its encapsulation, nor is it a plant which, compared to the seed, has attained its freedom. God as Ground does not destroy the causality of man, any more than the ground destroys the causality of the seed. On the contrary, just as the ground liberates the causality of the seed, enabling it to germinate, grow, mature and bear fruit, so God's causality liberates man's causality, makes man to be truly creative and make himself. Just as the seed alone grows, matures and bears fruit, not the ground, so man alone makes himself—he alone is reborn and achieves freedom.

Another analogy used by the Scriptures to explain divine causality is that between Bridegroom and Bride. Yahweh is the Bridegroom who liberates Israel (humanity) from her barrenness by giving her life, making her fruitful. Yahweh as Bridegroom does not destroy the causality of the Bride; rather, he facilitates the creativity of the Bride; he gives her time. It is the Bride alone who bears the child, who is pregnant, and who gives birth to the child. It is the Bride who has the time, who counts the time of her giving birth; the Bridegroom does not have time in this sense. So it is false to speak of God as History who is present to human history. God as Bridegroom, as Fullness of Time, as Ground, gives time, is the source of time, but this does not make him History as such, for he does not grow, evolve and have a history. Without the analogy we have furnished, if we merely think abstractly, we would easily fall into the fallacy of concluding that God is History because he is the source of time or history. God is the source of history without being historical, much as the Bridegroom is the source of birth for the Bride without himself giving birth or just as the Ground is the source of growth for the seed, without itself growing and bearing fruit. Just as the ground is not growth itself nor the bridegroom a mother, so God is not History, even if he is the source of time. God is the Ground of history. It is man that is historical, constituted by history through his interaction with God as Ground.

The next question with regard to human freedom is God's foreknowledge. It would seem that divine foreknowledge destroys human freedom. For how could man truly create and constitute history if it is necessarily known by God. It would follow that the future is not free, because God's foreknowledge would make it necessary. To answer the question, let us first consider the relation between knowledge and freedom. It is obvious that for there to be free choice there has to be adequate knowledge of the alternatives. Ignorance precludes free choice, and hence freedom. It is true then that, in a sense, knowledge makes us free; knowledge liberates. We can also say that the greater the knowledge, the greater the freedom, and conversely, the less the knowledge, the less the freedom. Knowledge in this case pertains not only to the knowledge of the object but also to knowledge of the self. If I do not know myself completely, then I do not know what is best for myself; my choice is not completely free. In the relation between man and animal, there is freedom in man because there is self-knowledge. Man can deliberate, can direct himself and throw himself into a project freely.

Having seen the relation between knowledge and freedom, let us now present a situation in which, let us say, one is in a large forest and has complete knowledge of all the exits. Then to say that there is someone who foreknows the path we are going to take out of the forest is to say that there is really no indetermination in the will. Free choice is destroyed. It will not do to say that the foreknowledge is not a cause of the choice. How can we affirm seriously that the will is undetermined if one can derive from it a knowledge of what it will do. If the will was not the source of the foreknowledge, where did it come from? From what determination? If the will is undetermined, then we cannot get any foreknowledge from it. Thus, in the way the question is posed, foreknowledge, if there be such a thing, does destroy freedom. The traditional explanations have not yet given an adequate explanation of how divine foreknowledge does not destroy human freedom. The solution to the problem is to get outside the hellenic framework in which the question is posed. Both the traditional view and the critics like Nietzsche, Sartre, etc., are within the hellenic framework.

It is false to relate divine foreknowledge to free will or free choice; rather, it should be related to man's lack of knowledge, and hence lack of freedom. In other words, we should start with man as unfree, as enslaved, not man as free. In the traditional view which sees man in relation to the animal, man is free, but in relation to his future essence which he must create, man is not yet free. He must liberate himself from entropy: from hate, from prejudice, from ignorance, from demonic forces in him. The presupposition of the Scriptures is that man is unfree; he is lost in the wilderness; he cannot find his way to the Land of Truth and Freedom. So he does not have free choice because he does not know. In this context, the knowledge of an expert guide who knows all the true exits, and dead ends, and the dangers along the way does not destroy the freedom of the lost wayfarer; rather, it liberates him, frees him from his predicament. To start with man as already free, as traditional thought and the existentialists like Sartre do, is to end up either depreciating human freedom as the traditionalists do to save divine foreknowledge, or denying God altogether to save man as the existentialists do. Again, we see here an excellent illustration of how the static pattern of thought has been the source of much of our false philosophic and theological problems, problems that have lasted for centuries and even to our day.

If we disabuse ourselves of such thinking, then we will see the obvious teaching of the Scriptures that man is unfree. He does not have full knowledge which is the foundation of freedom. As St. John says, we do not know yet what we shall be (1 Jn 3:2). Man is like a child who needs guidance, a wayfarer or pilgrim who has lost his way. God's foreknowledge is there to liberate him. It is in the context of man's ignorance and consequently lack of freedom that Christ was sent as the Way, the Truth and the Life. As Way, he leads us out of the wilderness of sin; as Truth, he liberates us from our untruth; and as Life, he conquers Death, the ultimate enemy of freedom.

Revelation as foreknowledge must be seen in the context of our liberation. Revelation is a light that aids the light of reason. It is a higher form of knowledge, a foreknowledge that tells man the unerring direction to the Land of Truth and Freedom. As the Scriptures say, the Truth (Revelation) shall make us free. Faith is also seen as a higher light than reason; it is the acceptance of Revelation. Now faith is a new dimension of being and of freedom, because in faith we die to sin and error which are portrayed as a state of darkness; we are reborn into the light; we are now sons of light. And having the light we can see our way around; we do not go about in darkness; we are free. The Scriptures also see God as a Father who must provide and foresee eventualities in order that humanity (his children) may be guided properly and helped toward maturity. The Father's experiences, so to speak, and foreknowledge do not destroy the child's freedom and creativity; rather they help the child attain maturity and consequently the exercise of responsible freedom.

The last question with regard to the problem of human creativity and the divine is that of divine laws and commandments which are claimed to restrict man's free constitution and determination of himself. Again, the difficulty here is a false one which arises only because we are trying to relate the divine imperative to a view of man as already free. Let us use our example again of the man in the wilderness who knows all the exits out of the forest. In this situation, for God to tell the man to use a given path rather than another is indeed to destroy the man's freedom of choice. It is in the context of the man lost in the wilderness that the divine imperative is to be properly understood. The commandments are rules of action that help a man who has lost his way, so to speak, to find his way out. In other words, he does not have the free choice of exits because he is ignorant of the exits. A guide then would not destroy his freedom; to tell him to take this way out if he wants to be free rather than that one which leads to a dead end is not to destroy his freedom because he is not free to begin with; rather it is to give him freedom. Or to use another example, a mother's advice or commands to a child are not meant to destroy its freedom but to help the child attain freedom and maturity. Once the child is grown up, and assumes full responsibility, then there would be no need for commandments. Similarly, as long as we are lost, as long as we are growing to maturity and freedom, we need guidance, commandments. But once we have achieved full freedom, it follows that all the forces of hate, the demonic forces of sin and death, are fully vanquished and conquered. Love takes over. Then we have the fullness of freedom. Then, too, there shall be no law, for as Augustine so well expressed it: *Ama et fac quod vis* (Love and do what you will). Then is man fully creative. But right now, man is not fully free. He needs guidance; else he destroys himself; he is not so much creative as destructive; everything he touches becomes a spoil of death. He is more an ally of death than of life. And yet we have men who think they are grown up, full creators of their own destiny, not needing the humility of childhood, of the ignorant, because man has come of age.

The Scriptures think otherwise. God's laws lead to life, to freedom. Thus, freedom has a structure, and this structure can even take the name of law: the "law of the Spirit of life" (Rom 8:2), the "law of freedom" (Jas 1:25; 2:12), "the pattern of teaching" (Rom 6:17). Without those laws, since man is not fully free, everything he touches turns to chaos, and freedom has nothing in common with chaos (Gal 5:13; Eph 4:14; 1 Pet 2:16). In the Christian view, the way to attain freedom is to follow Christ, so that in following his commandments one is "dead with him" (Col 3:3), "buried with him" (Rom 6:4), "raised with him" (Col 2:12), "lives with him" (Rom 6:8), "to be glorified with him" (Rom 8:17), "reigns with him" (1 Cor 4:8). The commandments of Christ are summed up in the law of love. The power of love to redeem and to free us comes from the celebration and commemoration of the eucharistic sacrifice which allows us to participate in the Christ events. The power of love allows us to come to know ourselves. It permits us to triumph over the forces of internal corruption, hate, sin and death. The power of love will extend into our bodies so that they too will be free from decay and corruption. And since our bodies are an extension of the material universe, material creation, which is groaning until now from its slavery to sin and corruption, as Paul points out, will also be saved. Man participates in Christ's priesthood in the salvation of the universe.

The Christian experience, then, is that man is in a state of slavery. For the non-Christian, it will have to be his own experience that will tell him whether the observation of Paul about human weakness and impotency is truer than the claim of those who believe that man has come of age and is able to achieve his own freedom. Whatever be the case, we cannot say with certainty that from an analysis of human creativity and freedom, God is a threat to freedom. Nor is psychoanalysis decisive in the matter, for it is not necessarily the case that belief in God is a projection of infantile needs and wishes; it could very well be that the desire to be free of all restraints and bonds is an adolescent and even infantile projection of the destructive forces of pride and hate that threaten to destroy the individual.

CONCLUSION

It would be fitting at the end of these reflections to mention the name of Teilhard de Chardin, for it is his evolutionary and processive view of reality that has most influenced my own thinking. I would therefore refer the reader to the published works of Teilhard as the source and inspiration of the work. I confess that, in the actual preparation of the work, it was a processive philosophy, which I have myself formulated from Teilhard's world-view, that directed and controlled my reflections.

While admitting my debt to Teilhard, it must be added that Teilhard should be absolved of any faults or inadequacies of the present study.

Teilhard has said that the success and validity of his thought can best be judged by how far those who follow him go beyond his thinking. I have tried to follow Teilhard but not in a slavish way. In fact, by the laws of development it is impossible to do so, for, inevitably, a true vital idea such as Teilhard's, as soon as it emerges in the noosphere, begins to complexify or differentiate itself. I would like to look upon my efforts as a process of differentiation or complexification of Teilhard's thought. Others who have been inspired by Teilhard have sought to reconcile his thought with traditional Aristotelian-Thomistic thought. The originality of Teilhard, I believe, was his effort to go beyond the traditional categories. There are others inspired by Teilhard who have applied his evolutionary and processive outlook to philosophico-theological problems. I belong to this group. However, even within this group, no two approaches are alike, for each one has approached Teilhard in his own unique way. The originality of my approach, if one can call it that, is to formulate a philosophy of process derived from Teilhard's world-view, which I have applied, first, to the problem of grace or the supernatural in my book *Teilhard and the Supernatural*, and now in the present study on the problem of God.

Let me summarize what I would consider to be the significant conclusions for the problem of God and unbelief derived from the application of a philosophy of process:

1. On the problem of method, the temporal rather than the spatial distinction between science and theology is a direct conclusion from processive thought. Theology in this case does not deal with supratemporal or timeless truths but with the eschatological (a higher temporal dimension of evolutionary time or process than the purely historical) and hence temporal truths.

2. Because theological truth and therefore theological language belong to the eschatological dimension, linguistic analysis as now understood and practiced which deals with empirical and historical truths cannot decide on the meaningfulness or meaninglessness of theological language.

3. Faith or belief is not supratemporal; neither is it existential, that is, outside the evolutionary process, for human temporality cannot be understood apart from the evolutionary process; it cannot be bracketed. Faith or belief is an evolutionary category. It evolved and is, in fact, the highest product at present of the evolutionary process. Because of this fact, the beginning of evolution may rightly be said to be the beginning of belief itself. Evolution is the evolution of belief.

4. The relation between reason and faith is not a spatial or static one but a temporal or evolutionary one. In other words, faith is not something superadded to reason from without in which reason is considered as perfect and self-sufficient in its own sphere. Rather, faith is the intrinsic perfection of evolving reason, its eschatological dimension. By the insufficiency of reason we do not mean to deny the "autonomy" of science. To do science, one does not need the help of theological or religious faith. But reason, taken in its totality—hence, not merely scientific reason, but reason in face of total reality—can never find the complete solution to human fulfillment in purely political, economic, technological or social means. Reason must attain the dimension of faith to seek answers to questions of ultimate import and which will not go away, such as the reality of God, the origin and destiny of man, the ultimate worth of human life, etc.

5. Reason is not neutral in relation to faith. It is structured for faith, instrinsically ordained to it. For reason to become fully itself, it must tend toward faith as to its fullness. But it cannot attain faith by its own powers, for it is much like an ungerminated seed which cannot germinate itself apart from its ground. In this case, reason as process needs a Transcendent Ground, for nothing in process is able to evolve itself apart from its ground.

6. Reason as "ungerminated," that is, as outside faith, cannot judge of the validity of faith in much the same way that an ungerminated seed or an unborn fetus has no idea, experience or "perception" of the reality of the seedling or of the born child. Just as the child justifies the truth and usefulness of the fetus, so it is faith that judges reason and not the other way around. But faith, it must be understood, is none other than evolved reason. Therefore, it is really reason judging itself, except that it is the evolved state of reason that judges

the unevolved state. Faith is not therefore irrational as some have claimed. Rather, it is the fullness of reason.

7. An analysis of the evolutionary process shows the need for its Ground as origin of growth, as sustainer of growth, and as goal of growth. We call this Ground of evolution "God."

8. Men who explicitly deny the reality of God i.e., relative atheists, but nevertheless affirm faith in the world and work for the good of the world, evolving it to a better state, implicitly affirm the Transcendent Ground of the world in process and therefore have some degree of faith. This conclusion implies a reevaluation of the traditional distinction between the Christian religion, on the one hand, and the so-called "natural" religions and atheism, on the other.

9. The Christian's goal of union with God is not a departure from the earth. For union with God as Ground of evolution means involvement in evolutionary time; advance into the future toward God-Omega is not a withdrawal from time but a fuller possession of it.

10. From a reformulation of God's eternity as Fullness of Time rather than as the absence of time results in a new understanding of theological anthropology. Thus, man is ordained for time. His reason is a gatherer of time such that the distinction between man and animal is not man's capacity to withdraw from time but the greater capacity of reason to gather time. Reason not only attains the past and the present better than an animal's memory and perception can, but it alone can attain the future by foresight, faith and hope. Faith, as the higher dimension of reason, is a power for the future that opens for us the Transcendent Ground or Omega of evolutionary time.

11. If God is the Fullness of Time or is God-Omega, it follows that the reality of God is better indicated by his

absence than by his presence. God could not be present in the present, for the present in the context of process is the region of the not fully real, the unfinished, the imperfect, the undeveloped. It is, in short, the region of unfulfilled time. Now, God who is the Fullness of Time cannot be in the present which is the region of unfulfilled time. For God to be present in the present is the same as for him to put an end to historical time. It would be the eschaton. Hence, in the historical present, God's reality is better indicated by his absence than by his presence. He is a *Deus Absconditus*.

12. Faith or belief in God is not the destruction of the freedom of reason but is its hope and guarantee. Freedom in the context of process is equated with fullness of being or of growth. For example, on the purely physical or biological level, it is evident that a normal and fully grown man is "freer" in the use of his hands, arms, legs, etc., than a child is. Thus, freedom, at all levels, is equated with the evolved, the mature, while unfreedom is equated with the immature or unevolved. Reason as immature, unevolved, does not have full freedom. It does not have full knowledge in which lies its freedom. Its hope of freedom and maturity is in faith. Reason, to use our previous example, is like an ungerminated seed— hence, encased, "bottled up," "unfree." Just as the ground is the source of the seed's "freedom" since the ground germinates the seed and gives it life, growth and maturity, so, too, God as the Transcendent Ground of reason does not destroy reason but liberates it. The "death" of reason, like the "dying" of a seed, is the birth of faith. Faith makes reason free.

FOOTNOTES

INTRODUCTION

[1] See his book, *Guide to the Debate about God* (Philadelphia: The Westminster Press, 1966), p. 101.

[2] Colossians 1.

[3] See Robert T. Francoeur, "Waiting for Teilhard," *The National Catholic Reporter Supplement* (Feb. 28, 1968), p. 9. See also his article, "The Compleat Teilhard?" in *The Critic* (Feb.-March, 1968).

[4] That transcendence is inherent in Christian thought is noted by Gordon Kaufman in his article "On the Meaning of 'God'," *New Theology*, 4 (Macmillan, 1967), pp. 71-72. Thus he says: "For the purposes of his 'demythologizing' program Bultmann defines mythology as 'the use of imagery to express the other worldly in terms of this world and the divine in terms of human life, the other side in terms of this side. But this leaves unquestioned the most problematic feature of mythological thinking: that there *is* an 'otherworldly' or 'other side' at all, which, in contrast with the 'human,' is viewed as 'divine.' . . . Demythologizing which fails to come to terms with the ultimate metaphysical-cosmological dualism expressed in the mythology, and in fact at the root, of all Western religious thinking, is not seriously facing up to the problem of irrelevance of the Christian church in contemporary life."

[5] Gabriel Fackre assesses the positive and negative points of the program of the "anti-transcendents" in his article, "Issue of Transcendence in the New Theology," *New Theology*, 4 (Macmillan, 1967), p. 193. Thus he says: "The anti-transcendents have said an important word. They remind us that the eyes of men are now turned to the human plane. Further, they have underscored the serious misunderstandings possible in our present conceptions of transcendence. What is properly a corrective, however, must be just that—a corrective and not a new gospel which merely accommodates to going notions and sensitivities." And speaking specifically of the death-of-God theologians, he says: "Proclamation of the 'death of God' is simply a theological version of the same megalomania which seeks to turn an old imperialism into a new one. Here there is no talk of God-man partnership or covenant dialogue, but the appearance of monolithic, monological man" (p. 189).

[6] Harvey Cox believes that the future of theology is lighted by two seminal thinkers of our time, Pierre Teilhard de Chardin and Ernst Bloch, and that the way out of the "death of God" miasma could very well be the processive and eschatological dimension in the thinking of both men. (See his "The Death of God and the Future of Theology," *New Theology*, 4 (Macmillan, 1967), pp. 248-49. See also his latest book, *On Not Leaving It to the Snake* (New York: Macmillan, 1967).

[7] See my book, *Teilhard and the Supernatural* (Baltimore: Helicon Press, 1966), Part II. Part of the reluctance to accept process thought is its association with Marxism in the minds of many. But evolutionary or dialectical thinking is not essentially Marxistic; it is intrinsic to the Bible. The type of evolutionary thinking that I use here is one that I have developed and elaborated from the world-view of Teilhard de Chardin. I do not claim that it was Teilhard's own. It is uncertain what Teilhard's philosophy was, for he never elaborated one. In fact, at one place Teilhard seems to explain evolution as the actualization of potency (see *The Vision of the Past* (New York: Harper and Row, 1966), p. 192n; at another, Teilhard recommends the transposition of the notion of the fixity of essence to that of genesis (from a letter of May 18, 1964; see Claude Cuénot, *Teilhard de Chardin* [Baltimore: Helicon Press, 1965], p. 369). But Teilhard was not a professional philosopher; the kind of philosophy implicit in his thought would have to be based on his work, not on what he said it was.

[8] See *The Divine Milieu* (New York: Harper, 1960), p. 34.

[9] The use of examples derived from the infrahuman level of evolution is a valid epistemological procedure in evolutionary thinking. The principle behind it is that of continuity according to which what is found at a higher level is also present at a lower level but in a form proportionate to that level. A specific example we will be using quite frequently to help us think theologically is that of the seed and its ground. The use of this example is justified not only evolutionarily but biblically. Thus in the Scriptures: unless the seed dies, it remains alone; if it dies it bears much fruit. Paul uses the dying of the seed and its rebirth to explain the theological meaning of redemption and resurrection, as in 1 Cor 15:37.

[10] See Max L. Stackhouse, "A Theology for the New Social Gospel," *New Theology*, 4 (Macmillan, 1967), p. 227.

[11] Johannes Metz observes how appalling is the unimportance of the future in theology. It has been forgotten to the point "that all modern theological discourse on the historicity of faith stresses only the relationship of the past to the present." He cites Bultmann as an example along with all existential theology derived from Heidegger. See his article, "Creative Hope," *Cross Currents*, 17 (1967), p. 172.

[12] For a fuller treatment see *Teilhard and the Supernatural* (Baltimore: Helicon, 1966), Part II. For some objections to process thought, see note to the Introduction.

[13] See David Jenkins, *op. cit.*

[14] *Ibid.*, pp. 56-70.

[15] *Ibid.*, pp. 71-81.

[16] *Ibid.*, pp. 82-88.

[17] Eric Mascall, in a review of W. Richard's book, *Secularization Theology*, in *The Thomist*, 32 (1968), pp. 106-115, says that "existentialist theology is out of harmony with what modern science tells us about man." He adds: "It is significant that for existentialist theology there are no problems about the relation between science and religion, for it ignores those facts about man from which the problems arise.... There is little sense of the Pauline assertion that the whole creation groaneth and travaileth awaiting redemption; rather it is man who groans and travails awaiting redemption from the world."

[18] See *The Phenomenon of Man* (New York; Harper & Row, 1959), p. 218.

[19] *The Phenomenon of Man*, pp. 283-85.

[20] See his book *The Theology of Hope*, trans. J. W. Leitch (New York: Harper & Row, 1967), p. 17.

[21] Metz, *art. cit.*, p. 173.

[22] The more philosophic objections to process thought are treated in Part II of my book, *Teilhard and the Supernatural*. The objections selected here were chosen because of their bearing on theology.

[23] See *The Phenomenon of Man*, pp. 86-90, where Teilhard speaks explicitly of "cellular revolution."

[24] Teilhard expressed the evolutionary view as "discontinuity in continuity." See *The Phenomenon of Man*, p. 169.

CHAPTER 1

[1] Walter Arnold, "Is There an Ethics of Belief?" *Cross Currents*, 17 (1967), p. 333.

[2] *The Phenomenon of Man*, p. 30.

[3] See *A Common Faith* (New Haven: Yale University Press, 1960), pp. 38-39. See also *The Quest for Certainty* and *The Influence of Darwin in Philosophy*.

[4] Eugene Fontinell, "Religious Truth in a Relational and Processive World," *Cross Currents*, 17 (1967), p. 300.

[5] *Loc cit.*

[6] Jürgen Moltmann, *op cit.*, p. 20.

[7] We are applying the law of continuity here, according to which "nothing could ever burst forth as final across the different thresholds successively traversed by evolution (however critical they be) which has not already existed in an obscure and primordial way" (*The Phenomenon of Man*, p. 71).

[8] *The Phenomenon of Man*, p. 167.

[9] See his book, *Types of Religious Experience, Christian and Non-Christian* (Chicago: University of Chicago, 1951), pp. 32-33.

[10] See his book, *Basic Modern Philosophy of Religion* (New York: Charles Scribner's Sons, 1967), p. 69.

[11] *Ibid.*, p. 65.

[12] *Ibid.,* p. 66.

[13] See his book, *The Sociology of Religion* (New Jersey: Prentice Hall Inc., 1966), pp. 14-16.

[14] See David Kingsley, *Human Society* (New York: Macmillan Co., 1948), pp. 531-33.

[15] See *Magic, Science and Religion* (Glencoe, Ill.: The Free Press, 1954), p. 90.

[16] *The Phenomenon of Man,* p. 167.

[17] *Ibid.*

[18] *Ibid.*

[19] *Ibid.,* p. 169.

[20] *Ibid.,* p. 168.

[21] *Ibid.,* p. 169.

[22] *Ibid.,* pp. 165, 171.

[23] *Ibid.,* p. 165.

[24] *Loc. cit.*

[25] *Loc. cit.*

[26] *Loc cit.*

[27] *Loc cit.*

[28] *Ibid.,* pp. 220-225.

[29] *Ibid.,* pp. 283-84.

[30] Mircea Eliade, *Myth and Reality* (New York: Harper, 1963), p. 11.

[31] *The Phenomenon of Man,* p. 284-85.

[32] We will leave to historians of religion the mapping out of the evolutionary development of religion: the first stages, the various branches the religious phylum took to evolve, the false steps, the dead ends and extinct forms, the viable branches, the leading shoot.

[33] F. Ferré, *op. cit.,* p. 81.

[34] See his book, *The Faith of Men* (Macmillan, 1967), p. 48.

[35] See Roger Garaudy, *From Anathema to Dialogue* (Herder & Herder, 1966).

[36] See his book, *The Faith of Teilhard de Chardin,* trans. René Hague (London: Burns & Oates, 1965), p. 173.

[37] See his book, *The Ego and the Id,* trans. Joan Riviere (W. Norton & Co., Inc., 1961).

[38] C. G. Jung has found from his lifelong work with peoples of both sexes and of different religions and cultures that at the level of what he calls the collective unconscious are invariable archetypal symbols: the feminine symbol and the child symbol. These symbols, he explains, signify the deep desire of the soul to give birth to something new, which is a process of liberation and individuation. Cf. his *Psychology of Religion* (Yale, 1938), pp. 1-77; cf. also Ira Progoff, *Jung's Psychology and Social Meaning* (New York: Julian Press, 1953), pp. 90-93, 194-97, 208-213.

CHAPTER 2

[1] Karl Rahner, "Atheism and Implicit Christianity," *Theology Digest* (Feb., 1968), p. 47.

[2] See "Constitution on the Church," section 16, in *The Documents of Vatican II*, ed. W. Abbott (New York: America Press, 1966), p. 35.

[3] See "Pastoral Constitution," section 22, Abbott, *op. cit.*, pp. 221-22.

[4] See "Decree on the Missions," section 7, Abbott, *op. cit.*, p. 593. See also comment of Rahner, *art. cit.*, p. 47.

[5] See comment of Rahner, *art. cit.*, p. 47.

[6] *Ibid.*, p. 45.

[7] *Ibid.*, p. 46.

[8] Matthew 25:31-40, in *The Jerusalem Bible*.

[9] See article cited.

[10] See Walter Eichrodt, *Israel and Its People* (Copenhagen, 1926), p. 308.

[11] See his *Economic and Philosophic Manuscripts* in Erich Fromm's *Marx's Concept of Man* (New York: Frederick Ungar Publ. Co., 1961), p. 127.

[12] *Ibid.*, p. 129.

[13] G. Kittel (ed.), *Theological Dictionary of the New Testament* (Grand Rapids: Wm. B. Eerdmans Publ. Co., 1964), p. 267.

[14] Genesis 9: 8-17.

[15] See *The New Bible Dictionary*, ed. J. D. Douglas (Grand Rapids: Wm. B. Eerdmans Publ. Co., 1962), pp. 264-65.

[16] Pedersen, *op. cit.*, p. 308.

[17] Kittel, *op. cit.*, p. 122.

[18] *Ibid.*, p. 111.

[19] *The New Bible Dictionary*, p. 98.

[20] Our attempt to show that the creation covenant is in the order of grace is important for our purpose, since we shall show later that an atheist of good will could appropriately be situated within this covenant.

[21] David Stanley, S.J., "The New Testament Doctrine of Baptism; An Essay in Biblical Theology," *Theological Studies*, 18 (1957), p. 179.

[22] *Ibid.*, pp. 179-80.

[23] *Ibid.*, p. 180.

[24] *Ibid.*, p. 178.

[25] See pp. 264-65.

[26] It might be further urged against our denial of the possibility of a natural knowledge of God that Vatican I holds that reason can come to know God (see Denzinger 1785, 1806, 2145). For example, it is stated that "Deum rerum omnium principium et finem, naturali humanae rationis lumine e rebus creatis certo cognosci posse" (D 1785). However, from a study of the commentary and deliberations of the Council, we find that what was being emphasized was that human reason was structured to know God, for its denial would imply the impossibility of knowing God at all. How reason comes to know God has not been defined by the Council. Gasser points out that the Council has left two things open: (1) how God is known from created things, and (2) how God's existence is demonstrated. The term "demonstration" does not mean logical inference, but must be taken in the sense of "cognition" in D 1785. But the

latter term precisely has been left vague by the Council (See *Collectio Lacensis* 7, 121).

CHAPTER 3

[1] The true search for God is to pray as if there were a God. The right attitude for the search is not to act the scientist or philosopher making conditions or stipulations for belief, but to act like a little child. This means that reason must not be taken too seriously, for it is underdeveloped.

[2] Incidentally, qualitative change is a Marxist notion.

[3] *The Phenomenon of Man*, p. 262.

[4] *Ibid.*, p. 51.

[5] We cannot emphasize often enough that these arguments for God's reality are not being presented as arguments based on reason alone. They are not meant to cause faith or belief in God. Rather, they are reflections proceeding from belief in God.

[6] *Ibid.*, pp. 218-19.

CHAPTER 4

[1] Schubert Ogden, *The Reality of God* (New York: Harper & Row, 1963), ch. 1.

[2] See *Letters and Papers from Prison,* ed. Eberhard Bethge and trans. R. H. Fuller (London: SCM Press, 1953), p. 164.

[3] See *Systematic Theology*, II (Chicago: University of Chicago Press, 1957), pp. 5-10.

[4] Ogden, *op. cit.*, p. 53.

[5] *Ibid.*, p. 15.

[7] See Roger Garaudy, *From Anathema to Dialogue* (New York: Herder & Herder, 1966), p. 95.

[8] See his book, *The Future of Belief* (New York: Herder and Herder, 1966), pp. 197-98.

[9] *Ibid.*, p. 195.

[10] *Loc. cit.*

[11] *Loc. cit.*

[12] *Ibid.*, p. 194.

[13] See *Teilhard and the Supernatural* (Helicon Press, 1966), pp. 153-58.

[14] See his book, *The Idea of the Holy*, 2nd ed., trans. J. W. Harvey (London: Oxford University Press, 1950).

[15] *Timaeus*, 37d.

[16] *Ennead*, 3:7,7.

[17] Physics, IV, 222b.

[18] *Ibid.*, 221a.

[19] See his *Dictionary of Theology,* trans. C. Quinn (Desclee Co., Inc., 1965), p. 144.

[20] See his *Christ and Time*, trans. F. V. Filson (Philadelphia: Westminster, 1950), p. 144.

21 J. J. Von Allmen (ed.), *Vocabulary of the Bible* (London: Lutterworth Press, 1958), p. 423.

22 Cullmann, *op. cit.*, p. 52.

23 *Ibid.*, p. 61.

24 *Vocabulary of the Bible*, p. 424.

25 Cullmann, *op. cit.*, p. 63.

26 *Vocabulary of the Bible*, p. 424.

27 *Loc. cit.*

28 See his *Old Testament Theology*, II, trans. D. M. G. Stalker (New York: Harper & Row, Publ., 1965), p. 99.

29 J. J. Von Allmen (ed.), p. 160.

30 *Loc. cit.*

31 *The Phenomenon of Man*, p. 166.

32 See Von Rad, *op. cit.*, p. 99.

33 *The Phenomenon of Man*, p. 88.

34 *Loc. cit.*

35 *Ibid.*, p. 105.

36 *Ibid.*, p. 107.

37 *Loc. cit.*

38 *Ibid.*, p. 106.

39 *Loc. cit.*

40 *Vocabulary of the Bible*, p. 160.

41 *Ibid.*, p. 424.

42 We must emphasize here that we are not absolutizing present time or just any future time. For our time is still lack of time. We do not celebrate twentieth-century forms and structures.

CHAPTER 5

1 D. Jenkins, *op. cit.*, p. 56.

2 *Loc. cit.*

3 *Ibid.*

4 Gabriel Moran, "The God of Revelation," *Commonweal*, 85 (1967), p. 499.

5 *Loc. cit.*

6 Moltmann, *op. cit.*, pp. 16-17.

7 *Loc. cit.*

8 *Loc. cit.*

9 Johann-Baptist Metz, *op. cit.*, p. 174.

10 Moltmann, *op. cit.*, p. 42.

11 *Ibid.*, p. 143.

12 George A. Buttrick (ed.), *The Interpreter's Dictionary of the Bible* (New York: Abingdon Press, 1962), p. 131.

13 *Loc. cit.*

14 John L. McKenzie, S.J., *The Dictionary of the Bible* (Milwaukee: The Bruce Publ. Co., 1965), p. 269.

15 Moltmann, *op. cit.*, p. 143.

16 John E. Smith, *The Spirit of Philosophy* (Oxford University Press,

1963), pp. 221-22.

[17] Linguistic analysis cannot develop as a discipline by ignoring ontology, i.e., a reflection on the nature of reality. Ordinary language cannot be a reliable starting point, for it is based on a Ptolemaic ontological view of reality.

[18] For a fuller discussion of symbolic language, see *Teilhard and the Supernatural*, pp. 204-06.

CHAPTER 6

[1] See his book, *A Philosophy of Man* (Monthly Review Press, 1963). The above quotation is taken from *Reflections on Man*, ed. Jesse Mann and R. Kreyche (Harcourt Brace, 1966), p. 305.

[2] *Ibid.*, p. 311.

[3] See *Thus Spake Zarathustra* in *The Portable Nietzsche*, trans. Walter Kaufmann (New York: The Viking Press, 1945), p. 397.

[4] See *The Future of an Illusion*, trans. W. D. Robson-Scott (New York: Doubleday & Co., Inc., 1964), p. 71.

[5] See *The Sacred and the Profane*, trans. Willard Trask (New York: Harcourt, Brace & Co., 1957), p. 203.

[6] See "L'existentialisme est un humanisme," trans. in *Existentialism from Dostoevsky to Sartre* (New York: Meridian Books, Inc., 1957), p. 289.

[7] *Ibid.*, p. 295.

[8] *Ibid.*, p. 303.

[9] *Loc. cit.*

[10] *Ibid.*, p. 290.

[11] See *Vocabulary of the Bible*, p. 250.

[12] *Loc. cit.*

[13] See pp. 130-31.